ELITE VOICES

Praise for *The Visibility Effect*

Janet's career visibility magic is practical, relatable, and energizing. A rich evolution from simple "personal branding," the foundation of her wisdom encompasses harnessing what brings you most alive as you move through the world, exponentially increasing not only your contributions and value, but the deep satisfaction available all along the way.

Tevis Trower, CEO of Balance Integration & Author of Game Changer's Guide to Radical Success

Driven by her passion to coach and mentor, Janet Wise delivers a bold invitation to professionals ready to step into the spotlight. With clarity and candor, she guides you from self-doubt to strategic visibility so you're not just seen and heard, but remembered. The Visibility Effect is your gateway to branding your brilliance and owning your rise.

Joanne Prifti, Senior Vice President, HR Americas

I send all my friends and colleagues to Janet when they're at pivotal moments in their careers—because she has this remarkable ability to spot the brilliance in someone before they see it themselves. So many professionals are busy doing the work, they don't realize how extraordinary they are, let alone how to articulate it, spotlight it, or leverage it. Janet changes that. She fast-tracks your career with strategy, clarity, and unwavering belief—and now The Visibility Effect puts that genius in your hands.

Ann Ward, Executive Presentation Coach, Ward Certified

The Visibility Effect is exactly what ambitious professionals need right now. Janet Wise has an unmatched ability to distill career strategy into bold, actionable truths and to deliver them with clarity and conviction. I've seen firsthand how she transforms professionals through her unique approach to branding and visibility. This book is not theory—it's Janet's proven playbook for accelerating careers.

Jim Hajny, Managing Director, Career Transition Operations, HR Partners International

Janet Wise shows that visibility is the decisive edge for ambitious professionals and distinguished leaders alike. I've seen her help countless executives amplify their voices, claim their value, and expand their leadership impact. The Visibility Effect captures that transformation and cements Janet as the definitive authority on career visibility™."

Gail Bigley, Executive Coach & Talent Development Executive for Fortune 100 Company

I have always been captivated by Janet Wise's perspective and insights on what it really takes to be seen, heard, and valued at the highest levels. Her multifaceted experience gives her a rare understanding of how ambitious professionals build thriving careers. The Visibility Effect upholds her hallmark of practical, actionable advice. If you're ready to amplify your visibility, this essential read will change the way you move your career forward.

Carol McClelland Fields, PhD, BCC
Business Mentor for Change Catalysts

THE VISIBILITY EFFECT

50 Truths to Accelerate Your Career, Your Voice, and Your Value

THE VISIBILITY EFFECT

50 Truths to Accelerate Your Career, Your Voice, and Your Value

JANET WISE, MS, HRD

ELITE VOICES

ELITE VOICES
San Antonio, TX 78229

First Edition, November 2025
ISBN: 978-1-63765-845-1
Library of Congress Control Number: 2025919934

Our mission is to empower individuals and businesses to enhance their professional brand by becoming recognized experts in their field. We provide the tools and resources to help our clients become authors, establish a strong personal brand, and grow their business to achieve greater visibility, credibility, and financial success.

Career Visibility™ is a trademark of Janet Wise.

For information, contact:
www.wiseadvantages.com

For the visible ones
—and those about to be.

Contents

This Table of Contents organizes the 50 Visibility Truths by the six pillars of the Career Visibility™ Framework, making it easy to spot what you want to act on now. In the book, they flow in order —read them straight through to build a visibility advantage that lasts.

Pillar 2: Communication —Message it so it matters.

Pillar 3: Presence
—Own the room before you enter it.

Pillar 4: Influence—Shape the conversations that shape your career.

**Pillar 5: Recognition—Make your impact
visible and undeniable.**

Pillar 6: Momentum—Visibility sustained is momentum gained.

Foreword

W hen Janet invited me to write this foreword, I said yes without hesitation. As CEO and chief learning officer of WeLearn Learning Services, an award-winning human capital firm with clients that include some of the world's best-known brands, I've had the privilege of seeing how learning can shape organizations at scale. Our work has been recognized with fifteen Brandon Hall Awards and Training Industry's Watch List for Custom Content Development, and is built on one belief: Learning changes people, and people change organizations.

That belief is also at the heart of Janet's work.

I first met Janet more than twenty years ago, when she was already making her mark in leadership development. Even then, she had a rare ability to see not only what people needed to learn but how they needed to be seen. That perspective shaped her career and, through her leadership, the careers of countless others.

Years later, over coffee in Chicago, I saw that vision expand in powerful ways. Janet shared the work she was doing to help ambitious professionals claim their visibility more intentionally. What began as early seeds of a wise idea had grown into The Branding Room™, The Career Visibility Studio™, and now crystallizes in the book you're holding.

Why does visibility matter now more than ever?

Because we are living through radical shifts: the rise of AI, hybrid work, and new organizational models. Technology is accelerating everything, but what sets us apart as humans is our ability to connect, to be seen, and to make our value visible and tangible.

That's why *The Visibility Effect* is essential reading—for individuals seeking growth, for leaders shaping culture, and for human capital professionals working to unlock potential.

Let's face it, talent development belongs to all of us: the individual, the leader, and the organization. And for those of us guiding learning at scale, visibility is the bridge between building capability and demonstrating impact. But its power doesn't stop there. The same approaches that make our function visible are the ones every professional can use to amplify their own career.

Career Visibility™ isn't optional. It is the currency of leadership, the foundation of influence, and the lever of opportunity. Janet has been advancing that truth for over two decades, and in *The Visibility Effect*, she delivers the frameworks, principles, and inspiration to not only understand visibility but to act on it.

Her work is practical, proven, and actionable. It equips you to step forward with clarity, confidence, and intention and to claim the visibility that accelerates not only careers but the organizations they power.

Sean Stowers
CEO & Chief Learning Officer
WeLearn Learning Services / Chicago, IL

Introduction

Visibility Changes Everything

T alent without visibility stalls. Hard work without visibility burns you out. Visibility is the ultimate career advantage, and in today's world, it's nonnegotiable. We are in an age of acceleration: AI reshaping roles, hybrid work blurring presence, and organizations reinventing themselves at speed. In the middle of this turbulence, one thing matters more than ever: being seen. Because no matter how good you are, if your work isn't visible, it can't open doors.

I've spent my career leading global learning, leadership, and career development functions across industries and Fortune 500 companies. I've been at the talent table, helping CEOs, executive teams, and HR leaders identify high-potential leaders and prepare them to deliver on the business objectives.

I've seen firsthand that the difference between someone who advances and someone who stalls isn't always performance. It's visibility.

As chief career and visibility strategist, I created The Branding Room™, The Career Visibility Studio™, and

Women in LeadHERship™, platforms that have propelled ambitious professionals into the rooms and roles that matter.

The patterns are clear: It takes more than exceptional performance to advance your career. It takes vision and visibility.

This book is for ambitious professionals at every stage, whether you're early in your career, in the messy middle, already leading, in transition, or stepping into an encore chapter.

And while visibility accelerates every career, it is particularly critical for women. Studies show women are promoted less often than men despite receiving higher performance ratings.[1]

That's not a performance gap. That's a visibility gap.

Career Visibility™ isn't a trend. It's a strategy. And it's the essential skill set for ambitious professionals who want to elevate, pivot, and lead with purpose.

Defining Career Visibility™

Career Visibility™ is the strategic ability to be seen, heard, and remembered for the value you bring—by the right people, in the right rooms, at the right time.

It's not about being loud. It's not empty self-promotion. It's about being intentional and being seen for the right reasons.

---

[1] Source: Harvard Business Review, "Research: Women Are Rated Better Leaders, But Are Less Likely to Be Promoted," 2019.

Why Visibility Matters

- 70% of roles are filled through networks and referrals.
- Women are promoted at lower rates than men, even with higher performance.
- Lack of visibility is one of the top reasons high-potential talent leaves organizations.

Visibility fuels:

- **Credibility**—People associate your name with value.
- **Mobility**—Visibility opens doors to new projects and roles.
- **Agency**—Visibility puts you in the driver's seat of your career.
- **Reputation**—Shapes how others talk about you when you're not in the room.
- **Leadership**—Builds trust, presence, and influence.
- **Engagement**—You show up more fully when you feel seen and valued.

How to Use This Book

Each of the fifty truths in this book is a bold, practical principle designed to accelerate your Career Visibility™. Here's the rhythm you'll find:

- **Visibility Truth**—A principle that shifts how you manage your career.
- **Career Visibility™ Move**—An action that puts the truth into play.

- **Reflect**—A question that pushes you deeper, aligning visibility with your goals.

Don't simply read these truths. Put them to work, capture notes along the way, test the moves, and pause to sit with the Reflect questions. This isn't just a book. It's a practice.

Because visibility doesn't change who you are. It reveals you. And that changes everything.

Before You Dive into the Truths...

Anchor yourself in the framework that makes them work.

The Career Visibility™ Framework:

Visibility isn't luck. It's a strategy. And like any strategy, it needs a framework.

The **Career Visibility™ Framework** is built on six pillars that every talented and driven professional needs. Together, they provide both the mindset and the methods to make sure your career isn't left to chance but is instead **seen, heard, and recognized by the right people, in the right rooms, at the right time.**

Success isn't the problem. You've already built that.

The risk is being so competent, so reliable, that your work speaks loudly, but your presence doesn't carry as far.

That's the narrow line between being respected and being remembered, and between being valued and being sought after.

Career Visibility™ is about closing that gap. It's where credibility becomes currency. Where your contribution doesn't only get noticed—it shapes the room, the conversation, and the opportunity. Because even the most successful careers can go **unnoticed or overlooked** without visibility.

These six pillars are the difference between staying in motion and creating momentum, and between being good at what you do and being unforgettable for the impact you make.

The Six Pillars of Career Visibility™

1. **Clarity:** When you name it, you claim it.
2. **Communication:** Message it so it matters.
3. **Presence:** Own the room before you enter it.
4. **Influence:** Shape the conversations that shape your career.
5. **Recognition:** Make your impact visible and undeniable.
6. **Momentum:** Visibility sustained is momentum gained.

THE
VISIBILITY
EFFECT

50 Truths to Accelerate
Your Career, Your Voice,
and Your Value

❝ The future belongs to those who are visible. ❞

VISIBILITY TRUTH 01

Visibility changes everything —if you know how to use it.

I didn't start my career at the top. I started as an administrative assistant. Later, as a learning specialist, I thought if I just kept working hard, someone would notice.

Then my company was acquired. Suddenly, the once-bustling fortieth floor of 60 Wall Street grew quieter by the day as leaders were picked up by the new team and peers disappeared into other groups. What had been a crowded, humming space became a nearly empty floor with a great view and a lonely future if I stayed invisible.

One afternoon, a female managing director walked over to me and said, *"You're smart. You're talented. But if they don't pick you, then pick them, because standing still isn't an option here."*

That was my wake-up call. I realized I had a choice: I could be invisible in the new organization, or I could be invincible.

That moment changed everything. It's what took me from entry-level to the global head of learning, leadership, and talent development at a Fortune 500 company. And it's the difference I've seen transform careers again and again.

You can be brilliant and still invisible, talented and still overlooked, and ready and still waiting.

Career Visibility™ is the strategic ability to be seen, heard, and remembered for the value you bring by the right people, in the right rooms, at the right time.

One client, a senior marketing manager at a global advertising agency, was delivering award-winning campaigns, but only her immediate client team knew it. Once we sharpened her story and positioned her wins in cross-functional forums, she was tapped to lead a high-profile global launch within months. Same talent. Same work. The difference was visibility.

Visibility bridges the gap not only between you and your next opportunity but between your potential and your recognition. It's the difference between *"Who's that?"* and *"We need her."*

Visibility isn't noise; it's not a brag post or another shiny update. Real visibility is intentional, strategic, and career-defining. It's about showing up consistently, memorably, and where it counts.

You don't have to become someone else. In fact, you become more of who you already are once you let the right people see you.

CAREER VISIBILITY™ MOVE:

Don't add work. Add visibility. Scan your to-do list, take one item, and share it with the people who need to see it.

REFLECT:

Where are you visible today, and is it shaping your future or simply keeping you busy in the now?

_____

_____

_____

_____

_____

_____

_____

_____

_____

_____

_____

_____

_____

_____

_____

_____

_____

" Have faith in
your luckiness. **"**

VISIBILITY TRUTH 02

Visibility isn't luck. It's leverage.

People love to say *"She just got lucky,"* as if visibility were some career fairy dust that landed randomly on a few chosen people.

But luck doesn't book the speaking slot or get you on the shortlist, and it definitely doesn't craft your message or advocate for you behind closed doors.

Visibility is a lever. When you use it strategically, it multiplies your impact. It activates relationships, accelerates access, and shifts perception.

Here's how luck plays out. One client I worked with was what I call a Quiet Star; her peers thought she was a quiet mouse doing her work with her head down. But what they didn't see was that while she stayed quiet with them, she was vocal and visible in the rooms that mattered. When a plum assignment in the London office came up, she was selected. Her peers chalked it up to "luck." In reality, she had been pulling the visibility lever all along.

The people who are visible don't wait for luck. *They create it.* They're intentional. They're focused. They're seen —on purpose.

Luck is often visibility in disguise. Believe you're lucky, act like the most powerful person in your own career, and you'll start to attract the very moments others call "good fortune." Your thoughts and your actions are the levers. That's what turns luck into career reality.

CAREER VISIBILITY™ MOVE:

This week, create your own "luck." Step into one room, one conversation, or one channel where you can be seen by people who don't already know your value.

REFLECT:

Where could you be using visibility as a lever instead of waiting for luck?

_____

_____

_____

_____

_____

_____

_____

_____

_____

_____

_____

❝ It's not about trying out—it's about standing out. ❞

VISIBILITY TRUTH 03

Don't wait to be discovered. Decide to be seen.

This is the trap I see the most with brilliant, high-integrity professionals. We assume that if we do good work, someone will notice.

But careers don't operate like talent shows. There's no scout waiting backstage to pull you into the spotlight. You may never see your name in lights, but you can put your accomplishments on a marquee. Every email, every update, every room you enter is a chance to headline your impact.

You're not an extra in a casting call. You're a leader with value to claim.

The moment you decide to be seen—not perform, not posture, but *seen*—you shift your career from passive to powerful.

Visibility doesn't require loudness. It requires ownership.

One leader I worked with had just delivered a project with big, measurable results. Instead of waiting for her one-on-one (the last two had already been canceled), inputting the data into the monthly dashboard, or like so many people, waiting for her next performance review as if that's the only stage where visibility happens, she took a different route.

She sent a brief follow-up email to her manager in real time. The subject line read like a headline, *"Cut delivery time by 30%,"* putting her impact front and center like a marquee. The email was opened immediately, her work was seen, and her manager was able to quickly share the win with senior leaders.

That one move multiplied her visibility across several rooms she wasn't even in. That's the Visibility Effect in action.

CAREER VISIBILITY™ MOVE:

Send one brief follow-up email about a recent accomplishment. Make the subject line a headline.

REFLECT:

Where are you still waiting to be discovered, and what would it take to put yourself in the spotlight?

_____

_____

_____

_____

_____

_____

_____

_____

> " You can't move forward by playing small. "

Stop editing yourself.
Start positioning yourself.

E diting is what we do when we're afraid of taking up too much space. We shrink the story, downplay the win, and keep trimming until we edit ourselves out of the story.

But positioning? Positioning is different. It's clarity. It's deciding how you want to be known and making sure that message is heard in the right rooms.

One client, a senior finance manager, used to "edit" every win. In team updates, she'd say things like, *"We just made a small improvement,"* even when her work saved the company millions. She thought she was being humble. In reality, she was shrinking back into her old role. She was a manager but kept speaking like a junior analyst, playing a smaller part than the one she'd already earned.

When we reframed her visibility, positioning her wins with clarity instead of qualifiers, she stopped sounding tactical and started showing up like a leader. By learning to *name* her impact and *claim* her results ("known for reducing risk exposure by 20%"), she shifted the perception in the room. She was invited into more strategic conversations and earned a seat at the tables where enterprise decisions were being made.

When you position yourself for where you are—and where you're heading—you become memorable for the right reasons, creating connection, alignment, and career momentum.

Stop cutting yourself down to fit into roles you've outgrown. Start showing up with the voice your role deserves.

CAREER VISIBILITY™ MOVE:

Take one recent accomplishment and strip out the "justs" and "onlys." Rewrite it as a "known for" statement and use it in your next email or meeting.

REFLECT:

Where have you been editing yourself, and what shifts if you position yourself instead?

_____

_____

_____

_____

_____

_____

_____

“ Busy isn't
the same
as visible. ”

VISIBILITY TRUTH 05

If no one knows what you do
—or why it matters
—it doesn't count.

Excellence is essential, but it's not enough. You can be outstanding at what you do and still be overlooked, outpaced, or underestimated.

Because visibility is translation. Your work only creates momentum if others can connect it to business impact.

Context is king. Alignment is queen. You've got to connect the dots and keep connecting them, because in organizations moving at Mach speed, even brilliant work disappears in the blur.

One director I worked with led a global process redesign that cut costs by millions. Yet in every meeting, her updates were reduced to "The project is on track" or a checklist of milestones. Her team knew the impact. People across the business felt it. But her boss, her peers, and the executive committee weren't connecting it back to business strategy.

And when those links aren't explicit, projects take on a life of their own—detached from the priorities that protect funding, visibility, and credibility.

So she made one shift. She stopped reporting activity and started translating impact. Instead of "The project is on track," she said, *"Our redesign reduced turnaround time by 40% —freeing up $3.2M this quarter."* Same work. Same project. But now it spoke the language of the business. She didn't walk in with a tracker; she walked in with a story. She didn't present a dashboard; she sparked a dialogue. And suddenly, she wasn't managing a process—she was shaping impact.

That's the power of translation. It turns technical speak into executive speak, makes excellence visible, and ensures your work doesn't just sit on dashboards but lives in the conversations that decide the future of the business... and your career.

CAREER VISIBILITY™ MOVE:

Translate one deliverable into business impact. Don't simply share milestones. Show how they connect to business strategy.

REFLECT:

Do you present work in your technical terms or in the language the business values?

_____

_____

❝ Résumés
land roles. Visibility
builds careers. ❞

VISIBILITY TRUTH 06

A résumé gets you in the door.
Visibility moves you down the hall.

A résumé lands the job. But once you're in, visibility keeps doors open and sometimes reveals doors you didn't even know were there.

One IT specialist I worked with was hired to keep help desk systems running smoothly. On paper, his job was uptime and troubleshooting. But he quickly noticed a challenge: Every time onboarding new hires dragged, the business lost productivity and credibility.

Instead of simply fixing tickets, he mapped the bottlenecks and built a streamlined workflow that cut onboarding time in half. He didn't frame it in tech jargon like "tickets closed." He translated it: *"New hires productive in 10 days instead of 20."*

That visibility changed everything. He realized his value wasn't only in tech—it was in solving business problems. He dove into process improvement, change management, and workflow redesign. He built a new suite of transferable skills and started applying them across the business. What began as an IT role grew into an entirely new career direction in business process improvement.

That didn't happen because of his résumé. It happened because of visibility. He kept his eyes open for where the business needed more, and he showed up to deliver it.

Your résumé starts the story. Visibility writes the next chapters, and sometimes, an entirely new career path.

CAREER VISIBILITY™ MOVE:

Look beyond your role description. Spot one business problem in plain sight and use your skills to help solve it.

REFLECT:

Are you only doing the job you were hired for, or are you spotting doors that could open your next career chapter?

"" You are the most important product you'll ever market. **""**

VISIBILITY TRUTH 07

You are a brand—and your brand deserves a visibility strategy.

You already have a brand. It's what people say about you when you're not in the room.

It's the labels that stick: "She's reliable." "He's the numbers guy." "She's the gatekeeper."

But here's the trap: Labels can shrink. They freeze you in an old version of yourself.

The standouts don't wait for labels. They reintroduce themselves with intention.

One receptionist I worked with was known as "the gate-keeper." She fielded customer calls, handled complaints, managed calendars, and kept the front desk moving. But she also had an eye for design and started building executive presentations. Because she understood both the *voice of the customer* and the *voice of the company*, she began positioning herself as communications support.

Soon, others stopped seeing her as "the gatekeeping receptionist" and started seeing her as the voice of the company. That intentional rebrand opened the path into internal communications and marketing, a career she hadn't even known was possible when she first sat at the front desk.

You're not your job title.

You're a full career story—and visibility is how you make sure others see the next chapter before they freeze you in the last one.

Strong brands don't change who they are—they pivot how they're seen, recognized, and remembered.

CAREER VISIBILITY™ MOVE:

Don't wait for people to "figure it out." Reintroduce yourself. Update your LinkedIn profile, your bio, or your intro in one meeting this week to reflect where you are now—not where you were.

REFLECT:

Are you letting old labels define you, or are you showing people the next version of brand you?

_____

_____

_____

_____

_____

_____

❝ Visibility isn't about showing off. It's about showing up in alignment. **❞**

VISIBILITY TRUTH 08

Visibility isn't vanity.
It's alignment in action.

L et's reframe the whole idea. Visibility doesn't mean performance. It means presence.

It's not about being loud. It's about being clear—clear about who you are, what you bring, and how others can recognize your value.

Showing off is about ego. Showing up is about alignment.

One senior leader I worked with used to hold back in meetings. She told me, "I don't want to sound like I'm bragging." She saw others taking up space, sometimes in ways that felt self-promotional, and decided silence was safer. But silence cost her influence. People equated her quiet with a lack of ideas.

When she reframed Career Visibility™ as alignment, sharing her perspective when it connected directly to business priorities, everything shifted. She wasn't performing; she was contributing. She wasn't chasing the spotlight; she was shining it where it mattered. And her voice became one of the most trusted in the room.

Too many brilliant professionals—especially women, especially mid-career—hold back. They wait to be tapped, chosen, or invited.

But visibility is rarely handed out. It's claimed.

You don't have to chase the spotlight, but you do have to step into it with intention and not apology.

CAREER VISIBILITY™ MOVE:

Identify one meeting or moment this week where your perspective aligns with a business priority and speak up.

REFLECT:

Where are you mistaking visibility for ego, and what would shift if you treated it as contribution?

_____

_____

_____

_____

_____

_____

_____

_____

_____

❝ Careers don't
just grow
—they're built. ❞

VISIBILITY TRUTH 09

Your dream career isn't discovered. It's designed.

L et's dismantle the myth that a great career is something you stumble into.

You don't find it—you build it. Not in one big leap, but brick by brick with clarity, courage, and visibility.

Most careers are shaped in the in-between moments: the decision to speak up, the quiet pitch in a hallway, the risk to stretch beyond your role, or the person who sees your potential—but only because you made it visible.

One manager I worked with was frustrated that her career had stalled. She assumed her leaders knew she was ready for the next step. They didn't. She never said it out loud. She never connected her work to her ambitions.

Once she started naming the impact she was driving *and* the direction she wanted to grow, everything changed. She wasn't just doing great work—she was shaping a path. Within months, she was tapped for a high-visibility project that put her on the promotion track.

Waiting to be ready is a stall tactic. So is waiting to be invited.

The people who rise aren't always the most talented. They're the ones who know how to move their career forward—even when the path isn't clear.

Career Visibility™ is the power tool. It helps you move with intention, not just ambition. It helps you get seen for who you are and where you're going.

You don't have to have it all figured out.

You do need to show up like someone who knows what they're building.

CAREER VISIBILITY™ MOVE:

Stop assuming your managers know your ambitions. State them. Then connect your current impact to where you want to go next.

REFLECT:

Where are you waiting for someone else to connect the dots in your career, and how can you start connecting them yourself?

_____

_____

_____

_____

_____

_____

“ Being known
beats being perfect. ”

VISIBILITY TRUTH 10

Perfection doesn't get you promoted. Visibility does.

You can be polished, prepared, and perform at the highest level—and still get overlooked.

Perfection is often invisible. It blends in. It waits until it's flawless before it speaks. It gets caught in the loop of "just a little more time," "one more draft," or "once I'm 100% ready."

But visibility? Visibility moves. It opens doors before you feel done. It speaks up even when your voice shakes a little. It shares the work in progress. It reminds people you're here, you're ready, and you bring value.

One manager I coached learned this the hard way. She spent weeks perfecting a proposal, determined to deliver it only when every chart was polished. In the meantime, a colleague raised a rough draft of a similar idea in a meeting. His version wasn't nearly as sharp, but it sparked the conversation, won attention, and got traction. By the time she finally shared her "perfect" proposal, the opportunity had passed.

That's the trap of perfection. Progress that's seen is more powerful than perfection that's hidden.

Mid-career, a COO mentor once told me something that changed everything: *Progress over perfection.* She wasn't telling me to lower the bar. She was telling me to move, stop hiding behind the illusion of perfect, and start leading with what I already knew.

People don't reward what they can't see.

CAREER VISIBILITY™ MOVE:

Share one idea, draft, or update before it feels "perfect."

REFLECT:

Where is perfectionism keeping you quiet, and what could shift if you let visibility lead instead?

_____

_____

_____

_____

_____

_____

_____

_____

_____

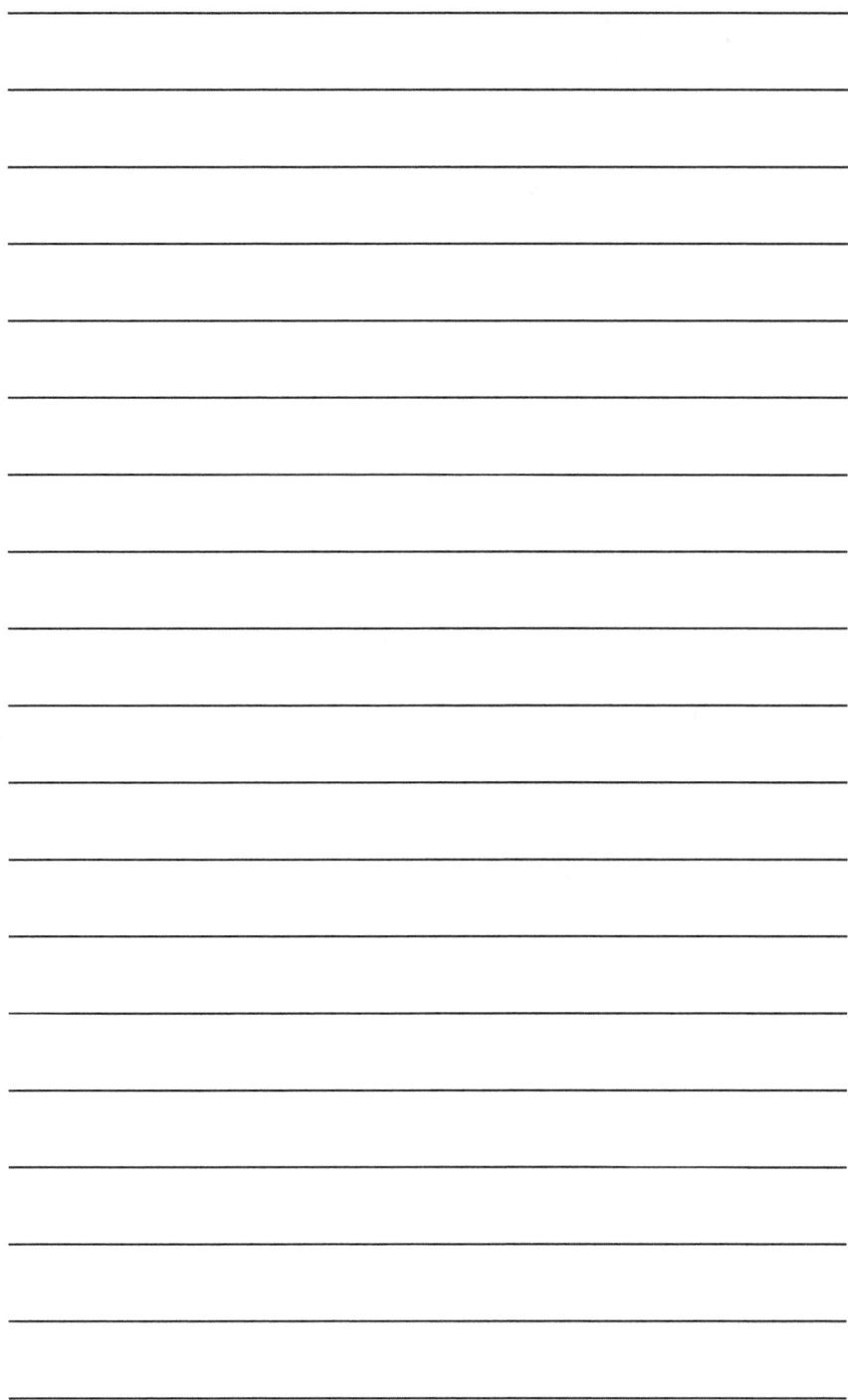

**" Clear beats clever
—every time. "**

VISIBILITY TRUTH 11

If your value isn't clear, your visibility won't stick.

We've all been there—trying to sound impressive, layering on jargon, and hoping it makes us look clever.

But clever can backfire. Clever confuses. Clear connects.

People aren't scanning for brilliance. They're scanning for relevance. They want to know who you are, what you do, and why it matters—fast.

When I was leading global learning and development, I worked closely with our chief marketing officer. What I learned from her changed the way I talk about value, forever.

She said, "The best messaging doesn't explain—it lands."

Think taglines. Think jingles. Think billboards on the highway.

The message isn't long. It's sticky.

That lesson showed up again with a client in a senior-level interview. On paper, she was impressive. In the room, she tried to wow them with complexity: frameworks, acronyms, and industry buzzwords.

The interviewer panel tuned out.

In later rounds, we shifted her talk track to one clear line: "I scale brands so they cut through noise and grow revenue fast."

That's what stuck. The hiring manager repeated it back to her in the offer meeting.

That's exactly what works in career moments too: the elevator ride with the CEO, the breakout session at a conference, or the unexpected moment when you suddenly have the floor.

If you can't articulate your value clearly, others won't be able to either. That's not only a messaging issue—it's a visibility issue.

You don't need a pitch. You need a pulse. You need a sound bite that speaks for you when you're not in the room—something clean, memorable, confident, and strategic.

Clarity isn't the opposite of clever. It's the result of knowing your worth—and how to speak it out loud.

Let's borrow a line from Bonnie Raitt: "Let's give them something to talk about."

Just make sure they're talking about your value.

CAREER VISIBILITY™ MOVE:

Write one clear sentence about your value—a line so memorable that others can repeat after hearing it once.

REFLECT:

If people summed up your value today, would it match the message you want carried forward?

" The best time
to build visibility
is before you
need it. "

VISIBILITY TRUTH 12

Visibility isn't a fire drill
—it's your insurance policy.

Most people treat visibility like a fire drill—only activating it when something shifts: a reorg, a missed promotion, or a job search. But visibility isn't a panic button. It's a career management practice.

Those who get tapped for stretch roles, plum assignments, or unexpected opportunities aren't always the loudest. They're the ones who invest in their visibility long before they need it.

When I sat at the talent table with senior executives, we often debated which emerging leaders were ready for bigger roles. Too often, managers struggled to articulate why someone on their team was ready—or worse, they failed to mention them at all. That didn't mean those professionals lacked capability. It meant they lacked visibility.

But when someone has been planting visibility seeds, sharing wins, building reputation, creating sound bites, their leaders can actually repeat—even the most tongue-tied manager can advocate on their behalf.

That's the power of strategic visibility; you've done the work and made it easy for others to talk about it.

Because when your name comes up behind closed doors, you want people to know: who you are, the value you bring, and the impact you deliver.

Visibility is a career asset. Invest early, nurture often, and reap the return.

CAREER VISIBILITY™ MOVE:

This week, plant one visibility seed: Share a win or best practice in a sound bite your manager (or peers) can easily repeat.

REFLECT:

What visibility habits today will your future self thank you for?

_____

_____

_____

_____

_____

_____

_____

" Visibility often
starts with an
unexpected opening
—and the courage
to step through it. "

VISIBILITY TRUTH 13

The right open door can make you visible before you're ready —and launch what comes next.

She thought she was home for summer break. Turns out, she was home for her big break.

My cousin was an art student at Syracuse in 1969. Tall, statuesque, and not looking for a modeling career.

But a photographer noticed her. He asked if she'd be open to a photo shoot. She said yes.

That one shoot—popcorn shirt, hot pants, *Village Voice* in hand—landed her on the cover of *LIFE Magazine*.

A cover seen by 8.5 million people. A career launched. A legacy defined. That image became iconic. It still resurfaces decades later.

But what's even more powerful? She didn't stop there. She went on to model professionally, then launched her own agency in New York and later in Europe.

She wasn't simply in front of the camera. She built the business behind it.

She hadn't planned it. But when the right door opened, she was willing to step through it.

And that step made her visible forever.

Doors don't open twice. Visibility is about stepping through when they do.

CAREER VISIBILITY™ MOVE:

Spot one unexpected door in your career this quarter and walk into it. Unplanned openings often become defining opportunities.

REFLECT:

Are you visible enough to be invited when opportunity knocks—and bold enough to step through the door?

_____

_____

_____

_____

_____

_____

_____

_____

_____

" Visibility
isn't what
follows success
—it's what makes
success possible. "

VISIBILITY TRUTH 14

Visibility is the outcome. It's the advantage that gets you there.

Too often, we think visibility comes after success. But professionals who advance don't wait to be recognized—they position themselves early, intentionally, and often.

One private client, a high-performing leader, wasn't looking to leave her company. But she was ready to level up. We refined her story, reintroduced her internally, clarified her value, and aligned it with where the business strategy was heading next.

Within six weeks, she was tapped to lead a high-profile initiative—before the opportunity ever appeared in the new business plan.

That's the power of visibility and *The Visibility Effect* in action. It puts you in the role before the role exists. Because it's not only about readiness—it's about awareness. When the business is shifting and repositioning itself, visibility is what lets you shift with it and be seen where it matters next.

CAREER VISIBILITY™ MOVE:

Identify one upcoming business priority and make your value visible in that space now.

REFLECT:

If the next big initiative launched tomorrow, would you be visible enough to be considered?

_____

_____

_____

_____

_____

_____

_____

_____

_____

_____

_____

_____

" Get in the room.
Then get
remembered. "

VISIBILITY TRUTH 15

Visibility isn't just about access.
It's about resonance.

I t's not enough to be invited. You need to turn presence into impact.

When I joined a global professional services firm as the functional L&D leader, I was surprised to learn I wouldn't be attending the upcoming global leadership conference.

It made no sense. This was a prime opportunity to meet my international peers, build visibility with the executive team, and align with the larger strategy.

But the response? Negative—the *budgets were already set.*

I made a business case anyway. I positioned it not just as a professional development opportunity but as a visibility investment for the L&D function and a clear ROI on their decision to hire me.

A few weeks later, someone had a scheduling conflict. They dropped out, and I was in.

Here's the part that mattered: I didn't just show up at the conference. I listened. I networked. I paid close attention to what the senior leaders were presenting, the strategies they were driving, and the goals they were setting. I remember it clearly even today—a $1.8 billion revenue target. Everything I delivered tied visibly back to those priorities.

And the following year, I wasn't just an attendee—I was a featured speaker.

That's what resonance does.

CAREER VISIBILITY™ MOVE:

Identify one closed door this quarter and make your case for why your presence belongs inside.

REFLECT:

When you are faced with a closed door, do you step back or make the case to get in?

_____

_____

_____

_____

_____

_____

_____

_____

_____

**❝ In times of change,
visibility is your
wise advantage. ❞**

VISIBILITY TRUTH 16

Reorgs don't just reorganize people. They reorganize visibility.

I see it all the time. And I've lived it—two economic downturns, two mergers, and a private equity buyout. Each one proved the same truth: In moments like these, visibility isn't about protecting your seat. It's about keeping your eyes wide open to where the business is going, your ears to the ground for what's shifting, and making sure your visibility and value match what's next.

Because the business and the marketplace will continue to shift—a reorg, a merger, a strategic pivot—and when they do, careers either rise or disappear.

Some professionals take a "duck and cover" approach, hoping to ride out the changes quietly. Wrong move.

As the business resets, the smartest professionals do the same. They tune into new priorities. They listen between the lines. And they ask: Where is this company going—and how can I help get it there?

Whether it's a shift in structure, leadership, or services, don't just protect your seat—position your value.

Because the leaders who get tapped next? They're already being seen as part of what's next.

CAREER VISIBILITY™ MOVE:

Don't just update your org chart. Update your visibility plan. Identify who needs to know you now.

REFLECT:

How is the business proposition changing, and where can you add the greatest value?

_____

_____

_____

_____

_____

_____

_____

_____

_____

_____

> **Momentum loves direction. Visibility provides both.**

VISIBILITY TRUTH 17

Momentum without direction is just motion. Visibility gives it purpose.

You can have the credentials, the track record, and the trust of your team, and still get stuck.

Because momentum alone doesn't move your career forward.

Visibility does.

I coached a leader with decades of results and glowing reviews. But she kept getting passed over for enterprise-level projects. Not because she wasn't capable but because no one saw her as a strategic voice.

So we took three steps:

- reframed her contributions in business language
- sharpened her leadership narrative so it tied to strategy
- positioned her so she showed up in front of the right rooms and decision-makers

One well-placed presentation and a follow-up email to the right audience shifted the trajectory. Before the end of the year, she was asked to join an enterprise transformation team.

Same leader. Same Skillset. Different visibility. Different future.

That's the difference visibility makes.

Momentum alone doesn't move careers. Visibility does.

CAREER VISIBILITY™ MOVE:

Pick one recent result. Draft a short recap (three to four sentences) that explains the *business impact* and share it with a leader who needs to hear it.

REFLECT:

Where are you working hard but staying unseen, and what story, told clearly, could move your value forward?

_____

_____

_____

_____

_____

_____

_____

❝ Visibility is how leaders scale their influence. ❞

VISIBILITY TRUTH 18

Visibility fuels leadership influence—especially when it's hard-earned.

Presence speaks before you do. It starts the moment people know what to expect when you walk into the room.

My client, a director of operations at a global logistics company, was leading a multi-million-dollar distribution upgrade.

And everything that could go wrong, did. Vendors missed deadlines. Critical systems failed in testing. At one point, a shipment was stalled for weeks, and trucks sat idle at the docks, losing money, wasting time, and shredding credibility.

He told me he dreaded every executive update. Each one felt like a minefield. One wrong answer and the entire project could collapse under doubt in his leadership.

Instead, here's what stood out: He didn't break. In every update, he was calm. In every briefing, he was clear. He never overpromised; instead, he gave people the next step they could count on, even when the timeline was falling apart.

He owned the narrative before anyone else could spin it. He got in front of the story and stayed there.

That was the first walk: presence under fire. And presence under fire builds trust.

Executives stopped bracing for bad news and started leaning in for direction. His managers echoed his words: *"We're on it. Here's what happens next."* People stopped asking *"Can he handle this?"* and started thinking *"Thank God he's handling this."*

Here's the second fire walk: Months later, another high-stakes transformation was announced. New systems. New deadlines. New risks.

But the shift in the room was immediate. He didn't have to reintroduce himself or prove his worth. Leaders weren't asking if he could deliver; they were relieved he was the one in charge.

The room already expected his presence. His influence arrived before he did.

That's the compound effect of visibility as presence. One project proved his leadership. The next project magnified it.

Visibility isn't about being noticed. It's about being known.

Presence under fire builds trust. Trust repeated becomes reputation.

And reputation? That's leadership carried in before you even enter the room. Because visibility doesn't just get you seen—it magnifies the influence you carry with you.

CAREER VISIBILITY™ MOVE:

Before your next meeting, write down one thing you want people to expect from you and then deliver it. Make presence intentional, not accidental.

REFLECT:

Are you consistent in how you show up, and how do you know?

_____

_____

_____

_____

_____

_____

_____

_____

_____

_____

_____

❝ Leadership without visibility is a hidden asset. ❞

VISIBILITY TRUTH 19

Visibility is leadership currency
—at every level.

You don't need a title to lead.

But you *do* need visibility to lead effectively.

Too often, capable professionals are doing all the right things—delivering results, mentoring others, contributing to the culture—but their value is tucked away in a file or buried in a slide deck.

Leadership visibility isn't about bragging. It's about clarity, consistency, and connection. It's about helping others understand who you are, how you think, and what you bring to the table.

Here's how I've seen this play out with first-time managers and senior executives alike. One private client—a respected team lead—was doing stellar work behind the scenes. But because she wasn't narrating her impact, key decision-makers didn't have her on their radar for a major promotion.

Once she started sharing key wins, refining her sound-bites, and aligning her message with business goals, things shifted. Her influence grew, and so did her opportunities.

Visibility doesn't only support leadership—it *accelerates* it.

It opens doors, earns trust, and scales your voice. Because the truth is people can't follow you if they can't *see* you.

Make your leadership visible before someone else defines it for you.

CAREER VISIBILITY™ MOVE:

What's one way you can showcase your leadership this week—in a meeting, message, or moment that matters?

REFLECT:

How visible is your leadership beyond your immediate team?

_____

_____

_____

_____

_____

_____

_____

_____

“ Promotions aren't
the only path
to visibility. ”

VISIBILITY TRUTH 20

Your next big career move might be inside your current role.

I worked with a corporate affairs director at a global consumer goods company who wasn't looking to leave her company. She liked her work and the prestige of her company, but she knew her career had slipped into autopilot. She was delivering strong results, but she felt something was missing.

She didn't chase recruiters or wait for a promotion. Instead, she made herself visible where she already was.

We started by refining her talk track, the words she used to describe her work, her transferable skill sets, and her vision for what she could do next. The goal wasn't to brag but to make her presence, and her potential, impossible to miss.

Then we focused on lateral moves, the kind of opportunities that shift perception without changing titles. She raised her hand for a cross-functional initiative. She offered insights in global meetings. She stepped into visible roles that showed her impact beyond her lane.

Lateral moves aren't detours. They're visibility accelerators.

And that's when things shifted. Suddenly, senior leaders weren't only seeing her as reliable in her role—they were seeing her as ready for more. The lateral moves reframed her value and expanded her influence.

Lateral experiences don't only build breadth of expertise. They expand the rooms you're visible in, and that's where influence grows.

She didn't change her title. She didn't change her company. She changed her visibility. And that changed her trajectory and her engagement.

Promotions aren't the only path to visibility.

CAREER VISIBILITY™ MOVE:

Identify one lateral move—cross-functional project, stretch assignment, or visible collaboration—that could expand how others see your value. Don't wait to be tapped. Raise your hand now.

REFLECT:

When was the last time a decision-maker in your company learned something new about what you're capable of?

_____

_____

_____

_____

_____

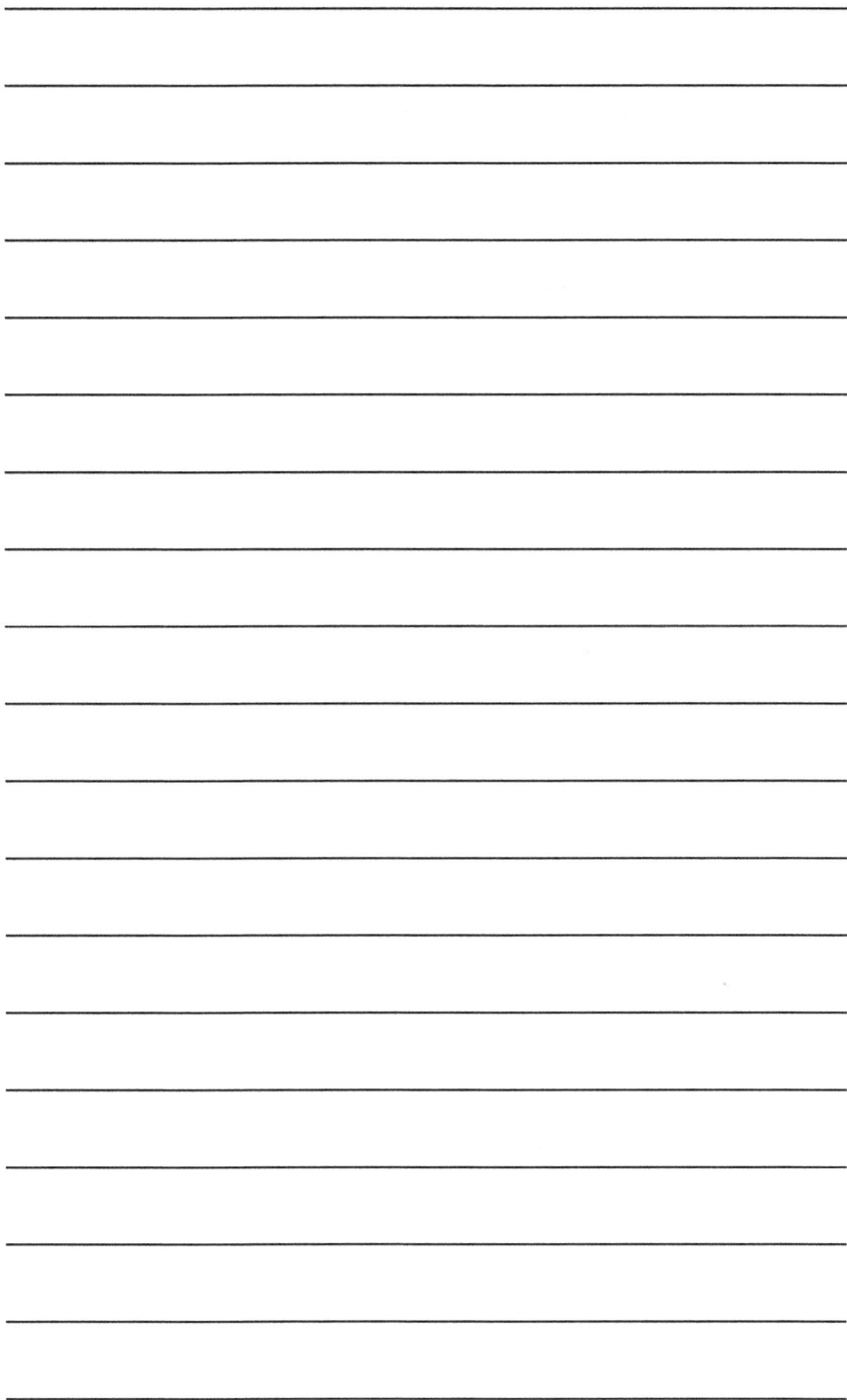

"Even the brightest lights burn out if they never recharge."

Visibility isn't sustained by constant motion—it's sustained by renewal.

The best leaders don't grind themselves or their brands into exhaustion. They know momentum is built not only in the moves they make but in the pauses that prepare them for the next one.

I have a friend who was known for flawless delivery. She was always on, always the one who could be counted on —and not just at work but on the home front too. She did it all. But after years of nonstop visibility, her presence lost its edge.

Instead of pushing harder, she took a strategic pause, stepping away from external panels for six months to focus on a global project that stretched her thinking.

When she re-emerged, she wasn't just reliable. She was revitalized, bringing new insights, new language, and a stronger voice.

She didn't lose visibility. She leveled it up.

And I've seen this play out globally. While American leaders cling to their two weeks of vacation in August, my international counterparts actually unplug for longer. Europe goes quiet, and leaders travel, recharge, and return stronger. Even Bill Gates famously took "Think Weeks," retreating with nothing but books and notebooks to reset his perspective. Renewal isn't indulgence—it's visibility strategy.

Here's how it plays out:

Burnout makes you disappear. Renewal makes you unforgettable.

Visibility isn't about being everywhere. It's about coming back with something worth seeing.

Don't just manage your calendar—manage your energy.

CAREER VISIBILITY™ MOVE:

Identify one place where you're over-visible and step back. Use that space to reset. When you reenter, bring something new that refreshes your presence.

REFLECT:

Where could a pause sharpen your visibility instead of dimming it?

_____

_____

_____

_____

_____

_____

❝The right question can be your most visible moment.❞

VISIBILITY TRUTH 22

A question can do more for your visibility than a dozen answers.

S ilence blends in. Questions stand out.

A director I worked with was already well-respected in his company. His projects were delivered on time, his team liked him, and his performance reviews were solid. Yet, in large high-level meetings, he was invisible.

He'd sit quietly through discussions, waiting for a topic that connected directly to his work. One day, he admitted, "By the time I think of something to say, the conversation has already moved on."

I suggested he shift the focus. Instead of searching for the perfect contribution, we started preparing two or three thoughtful, open-ended questions before every meeting.

Sometimes they were context-driven: "How will this align with the other initiatives launching this quarter?"

Sometimes they were forward-looking: "What's the one thing that could derail this plan in the next six months?"

And sometimes, they came at that moment when leadership asked, "Any questions?" a moment he used to let pass in silence.

These questions weren't combative or self-serving; they were invitations to think, engage, and explore. They positioned him as someone curious, invested, and thinking beyond his lane. Over time, people started looking toward him when complex topics came up, not because he had all the answers but because he asked the questions that moved the conversation forward.

The most visible people in the room aren't the ones with answers. They're the ones with the questions no one else thought to ask.

CAREER VISIBILITY™ MOVE:

Before your next meeting, prepare one open-ended question that invites dialogue and shows you're engaged in the bigger picture, and be ready to ask it when the floor opens.

REFLECT:

When the opportunity to speak comes up, are you ready, or do you stay silent?

_____

_____

_____

_____

_____

_____

" Your last
question is
your lasting
impression. **"**

VISIBILITY TRUTH 23

The right question can get you hired before you walk out the door.

I n meetings, the right question shows you're engaged. In interviews, the right questions show you belong.

An account manager at a creative agency came to me before interviewing for a senior client-facing role. She knew the basics—show her portfolio, walk through her wins, and build rapport. But when we got to the end-of-interview moment, I asked what she planned to say when they inevitably asked "Do you have any questions for us?"

Her first thought? "What's the culture like?" or "What are the next steps?" Safe. Polite. Completely forgettable. Worse—they were the kind of questions you could answer with a quick Google search or by reading the job posting.

We flipped the script. I told her, "That's not a closing question—that's small talk. Your last question should make them see you in the role before you've even got it." She prepared targeted questions that connected to the agency's clients, creative process, and growth goals.

- "What would success for this role look like by the time the agency's biggest campaign of the year launches?"
- "What's one opportunity with your current client portfolio you'd love to see the person in this role pursue?"
- "When a client project hits a wall, what do your best account managers do differently to move it forward?"

When the interview came, she used one of those questions in the final minutes. It sparked a conversation about the agency's biggest client challenge, and it turned into an impromptu brainstorm where she got to showcase her thinking on the spot.

A week later, she had the offer. One of the hiring managers told her, "We could see you in the seat before you walked out the door."

Interviews don't end with your answers. They end with your questions, and that last one can seal the deal.

CAREER VISIBILITY™ MOVE:

Don't waste your last question. Close with a question that signals you're already thinking like an insider.

REFLECT:

If your final question is the last thing they remember about you, what picture will it leave in their minds?

_____

_____

_____

“ Tenure gets respect. Relevancy gets results. ”

VISIBILITY TRUTH 24

Past performance doesn't guarantee future opportunity. Relevance does.

I n one of my fractional leadership roles, I met a senior executive who had been with the company for over two decades. He had a track record of big wins, a loyal team, and an enviable network. But lately, he was getting bypassed for the most innovative projects—the kind that were shaping the company's future.

When we talked, it became clear why: He was still working from his "greatest hits" list.

His résumé was full, but his relevance was fading. He was known for what he *had* done, not for what he was doing now.

We worked on shifting his visibility from legacy to relevancy. He started showing up in new spaces, contributing to discussions on emerging trends, taking the lead on pilot programs, and making his learning visible. Soon, he wasn't just the guy who *had* delivered; he was the one people looked to for what was next.

It's easy to think your history will carry you, but the truth is, no one's buying yesterday's headlines.

Visibility isn't about yesterday's headlines—it's about making today's work impossible to overlook.

Relevance is the real promotion.

CAREER VISIBILITY™ MOVE:

Identify one current trend, tool, or challenge in your industry and take a visible role in addressing it.

REFLECT:

If people only knew you from the last ninety days, would they see you as relevant?

_____

_____

_____

_____

_____

_____

_____

_____

_____

_____

_____

❝ When you learn
with intention,
you're not only
building skills.
You're building
visibility. **❞**

VISIBILITY TRUTH 25

Intentional learning is your career advantage. Apply it, leverage it, let it be seen.

Everyone's learning. But only a few are doing it with intention—and those are the ones getting noticed.

They're not only staying relevant. They're becoming indispensable. They're not only growing. They're being seen growing. And that changes everything.

Intentional learners don't wait to be developed. They seek, stretch, and connect because they operate from two powerful internal drivers: growth and curiosity.

They believe they can evolve. They ask questions and challenge themselves. And they do it in ways others can see.

It's not about knowing more—it's about showing up with a mindset that says: I'm in motion. I'm open. I'm ready.

And when others see that? They respond—with opportunities, with access and with belief.

One manager in a global leadership program put this into action. After each session, he shared a short update on the company's collaboration platform: what he'd learned, why it mattered, and exactly how he planned to apply it with his team.

These weren't long posts, but they were specific, and they reached leaders far beyond his immediate circle.

A few months later, when the company announced a major merger, he was invited to join the merger integration task force.

Not because he was the loudest voice in the room, or the most tenured. But because people had already seen him applying new ideas in real time.

That visible application signaled growth and made his visibility undeniable. That's what gets you tapped for what's next.

Because behind every professional leap is someone who paused to ask, reflect, learn, and stretch.

Intentional learners stand out because they:

- ask better questions
- connect across silos
- absorb feedback without fear
- adapt fast—and visibly
- position themselves as strategic contributors

In flattened orgs, fast-changing industries, and hybrid workplaces, Career Visibility™ doesn't happen by default. It happens by design.

Intentional learners lead with it—their careers reflect it. And their visibility proves it.

CAREER VISIBILITY™ MOVE:

Pick one insight from your latest learning and put it into play. Act fast and let others see it in motion.

REFLECT:

What have you learned—and made visible—in the last month that proves your value and visibility?

_____

_____

_____

_____

_____

_____

_____

_____

_____

_____

_____

_____

66 Think like
the understudy,
ready to own
the stage, because
every spotlight is a
visibility moment. 99

VISIBILITY TRUTH 26

High-stakes moments don't give you a heads-up—they give you a spotlight.

And in that spotlight, your visibility is either accelerated … or forgotten.

Psychologist Carol Dweck's research on growth mindset shows that people who see challenges as opportunities, not threats, are the ones who excel under pressure. They don't panic when the stakes rise; they perform.

That's exactly what happened to a senior account director at a creative agency. The client pitch was worth millions. Her boss, the closer, was set to lead. An hour before the meeting, he called from the airport: stuck. She stepped in. And she nailed it.

Here's why:

- **Preparation:** She'd done her homework, even though she wasn't "supposed" to lead. She knew the client's current campaigns, their biggest competitive threat, and the metrics that mattered most.

- **Mindset:** She saw this as an opening, not a trap. The runner-up was ready to run.
- **Style:** She didn't try to mimic her boss's delivery. She led with her own voice, building connection over a shared industry challenge.
- **Composure:** She used the adrenaline as fuel, stayed grounded, and answered every curveball without flinching.

Two weeks later, the agency landed the account, and the client requested her as the lead going forward. Inside the agency, she went from "solid" to "standout" in one meeting.

One spotlight moment can propel you forward or keep you waiting offstage.

Visibility accelerators don't simply measure performance. They rewrite reputation.

CAREER VISIBILITY ™ MOVE:

What's your next high-stakes moment? It may come without warning. Prepare now so when the spotlight finds you, you're ready.

REFLECT:

If your name were called to step in tomorrow, would you be the understudy ready to deliver or the one still flipping through the script?

_____

_____

" Not everything
that gets you seen
moves you forward. **"**

VISIBILITY TRUTH 27

Visibility without principles isn't strategy. It's a liability.

Remember the concert video that went viral—the one with a CEO and a chief people officer caught on the Kiss Cam? The clip was shared, dissected, and judged in seconds. The fallout was instant.

This wasn't just a social media scandal. It was a masterclass in what happens when visibility isn't grounded in values. In today's world, you are always on the record ... and on the fan cam. Every meeting. Every message. Every moment.

I've seen the same thing play out in the professional world.

A senior leader I worked with built years of credibility, until one careless LinkedIn comment came off as dismissive of a competitor. It spread quickly across the industry, and her reputation took the hit. She wasn't remembered for her expertise but for that one tone-deaf remark.

The real question isn't "How do I get seen?" It's "What story does my presence tell even when I think no one's watching?"

And even more critically: "Are my values clear enough to hold up under the spotlight?"

Because not everything that gets you seen moves you forward, and the wrong kind of visibility leaves a mark—in lost trust, in strained teams, and in the quiet meetings you're no longer invited to.

The moment ends. The perception stays.

When visibility isn't anchored in values, it doesn't accelerate you. It erases you.

CAREER VISIBILITY™ MOVE:

Audit your digital and in-person presence for alignment with your values. Before you hit send or step into the room, ask, "If this moment went public, would it strengthen or weaken my credibility?"

REFLECT:

When was the last time you were visible without meaning to be? Did it reinforce the leader you want to be remembered as or work against it?

_____

_____

_____

_____

_____

_____

❝ Rest is a visibility move—because no one remembers burnout as your best look. ❞

VISIBILITY TRUTH 28

Burnout doesn't just drain you. It makes you less visible.

We've all been there: logging onto a Zoom and watching a professional show up distracted, frazzled, or drained. The words may be fine, but the presence is off. And you can feel it.

A Rice University study found that remote professionals actually take fewer breaks and often work longer hours trying to prove productivity. The result? Burnout creeps in fast, and it shows.

That's the danger: Burnout doesn't only live inside you. It leaks into the way others see you. It shows up in the rushed delivery, the glazed-over stare, and the lack of edge in your voice. And it chips away at your credibility long before you realize it.

The irony? Professionals often over-prepare the slides and under-prepare themselves. No deck can cover up exhaustion. People don't remember your PowerPoint. They remember your power—or the lack of it.

I've seen the opposite too: a VP who paused before logging in, took a breath, reset his energy, and entered calm and clear. The updates were routine, numbers, status, the usual.

But the visibility was powerful. One left the impression of being scattered.

The other? Steady, credible, and trusted.

Visibility isn't just about being there. It's about how you show up. If you're running on fumes, the room will notice, and they'll remember.

According to the American Psychological Association, 62% of professionals say intentional breaks improve resilience, creativity, and decision-making. Translation: Pauses don't slow you down—they keep your presence sharp and visibility on point.

Because, as one senior leader told me, "You've got to go slow to go fast."

The deck informs. Your presence persuades. Yes, content matters, but visibility carries it.

CAREER VISIBILITY™ MOVE:

Audit your last three Zooms. Were you energized, prepared, and present or just surviving? If you'd cringe at the replay, it's time to reset before your brand pays the price.

REFLECT:

What signal is your visibility sending when you're stretched too thin?

_____

_____

" The best view
comes after
the hardest climb. **"**

VISIBILITY TRUTH 29

Momentum is made in the climb, not gifted at the peak.

M ost people wait for momentum to arrive in the big moment: the pitch, the promotion, or the presentation.

But real momentum is built in the stretch before you're ready, in the part no one talks about: the climb.

I recently rode a century-old wooden roller coaster. It didn't glide; it climbed. Slowly. Relentlessly.

Every inch felt like nothing was happening … until everything was.

Careers are like that. The visible wins, the "top," are never the start of your momentum. They're the result of the quiet, consistent work you put in before anyone's watching—the late-night prep, the follow-up no one expected, or the skill you mastered before it was trendy.

That's the climb that builds trust, influence, and opportunity, and it's where momentum really starts. Don't hide your climb. Let the right people see your progress.

Show the steps, not just the summit, because decision-makers don't bet on the summit. They bet on the climb.

CAREER VISIBILITY™ MOVE:

Share one "click" of your climb this week—a skill you're sharpening, a step you've taken, or a win in progress—so decision-makers see you already in motion.

REFLECT:

What part of your climb are you in right now, and who can see it?

_____

_____

_____

_____

_____

_____

_____

_____

_____

_____

_____

_____

“ The crack
in your story
might be the
most compelling
part of you. ”

Career visibility isn't about hiding the breaks—it's about showing the gold you've built through them.

Years ago, I wrote about *Wabi-Sabi*, the Japanese philosophy that honors the beauty of imperfection.

Later, I discovered *Kintsugi*, the art of repairing broken pottery by filling its cracks with shimmering gold.

The flaws don't disappear. They're illuminated, made visible, and made valuable.

Perfection doesn't inspire. Transformation does.

I've refinished old furniture the same way—not erasing its history but embracing it. The chips, dents, and layers of paint told the story of where it had been, and the transformation told the story of where it was going.

Careers are like that. They're not flawless arcs. They're shaped by breaks and detours:

- the layoff that redefined your priorities
- the pivot you didn't see coming

- the burnout that demanded a reset
- the promotion you were passed over for ... until it lit a fire under you

These aren't disqualifiers. They're career-defining moments. They're the parts of your story that reveal who you are—and what you've built from it.

The professionals who own those cracks and articulate the gold they mined don't only gain respect. They gain visibility—kind that's earned and unforgettable.

The cracks don't weaken your story. They make it shine.

CAREER VISIBILITY™ MOVE:

Identify one challenge in your career that shaped you. Write down the lesson, the strength, and the edge it gave you. That's gold you can share in interviews, presentations, or leadership conversations.

REFLECT:

If someone only knew your "perfect" career story, what defining edge would they miss?

_____

_____

_____

_____

_____

❝ Resistance isn't a red flag. It's proof you're playing bigger. ❞

VISIBILITY TRUTH 31

Staying safe won't get you seen. And it won't move you forward.

The Sticky Place is a term coined by Price Pritchett, PhD. It's when you've done the hard part and decided to stretch, apply, ask, be seen, and tell the truth about what you want next. And now?

Everything feels sticky. Uncertain.

You second-guess yourself. You wonder if you're "too much" or "not enough." Even the people closest to you start offering resistance disguised as concern.

It's not a failure. It's a threshold. Resistance doesn't mean you're off course. It usually means you're on it.

Your biggest obstacle isn't the job market or the organizational politics keeping you in place. It's your internal resistance to being seen differently. And that resistance can look like:

- avoiding the LinkedIn post that would raise your profile
- taking weeks to update your résumé or bio
- shrinking your ask in negotiations

- accepting less-than-aligned offers out of fear, not fit
- waiting for "one more" credential before declaring your expertise

It's not laziness. It's neuroscience.

Uncertainty and visibility can trigger the same alarms in your brain as physical danger. And while some will cheer you on, others may hesitate. Sometimes it's protection. Sometimes it's projection.

Don't mistake their fear for your facts. Name it. Resistance is normal. Call it out so it loses power. Reframe it. Discomfort means you're expanding, not regressing.

Act anyway. You don't need to be ready; you need to be real. Clarity comes through motion.

According to Gallup©, professionals who regularly seek visibility and feedback are three times more likely to experience career advancement over twelve months.

That means showing up before you feel 100% confident isn't reckless—it's a visibility strategy.

CAREER VISIBILITY™ MOVE:

Pick one action you've been delaying because it feels uncomfortable—and make it now. Visibility expands when you push through the stickiness.

REFLECT:

Where are you holding back because it feels safer, and what's the story you're telling yourself that keeps you there?

" Reinvention
is optional.
Reintroduction
is powerful. "

VISIBILITY TRUTH 32

You don't have to start over. You have to show up again.

Reinvention gets all the headlines. But most careers don't pivot on total transformation—they evolve. And sometimes, that evolution deserves a deliberate reintroduction.

One client, a healthcare recruiter, once spent her days filling clinical roles. After leading an enterprise technology integration project for her hospital system, she became the go-to resource for the talent acquisition team—working at the intersection of technology and talent.

She didn't become a different person. She didn't even change industries.

But her next chapter required a different introduction. Her visibility shifted with one deliberate reintroduction.

No longer just "the recruiter," she became known as: Transforming Talent Operations in Healthcare, a Program Manager Aligning People & Performance.

Now, instead of being seen only as "the recruiter," she's recognized as a dedicated program manager with expertise in clinical recruitment, scalable solutions, and the strategic integration of modern technologies for talent optimization in value-based healthcare.

Not a reboot. Not a reinvention. A confident reappearance. With elegance, visibility, and timing that says "My story and value still matter."

She didn't change the core. She re-entered the narrative anchored in what made her unforgettable in the first place— just refreshed for this moment.

And she's not alone.

In 2024, nearly 60% of professionals said they were exploring new opportunities, but for many, the goal wasn't to start over. It was to be seen again, in the context of who they've become.

It's not about pivoting everything. It's about staying visible and relevant; in step with what the moment, your employer, and the marketplace call for, so the right people see you, remember you, and reach out to you.

Because visibility isn't about starting over. It's about showing up—again.

CAREER VISIBILITY™ MOVE:

Audit your digital introduction: your LinkedIn headline, online bio, email signature, even the way you introduce yourself in virtual meetings. Update it to reflect who you are now and the value you deliver.

REFLECT:

If you reintroduced yourself today, without changing your core, what would you want the right people to see, remember, and reach out to you for?

❝ You don't just need a seat at the table. You need the right people at it. ❞

VISIBILITY TRUTH 33

No one gets visible in a vacuum.

Think of your career as a business. Every successful business has a leadership team—experts in finance, legal, operations, technology, and communication —who guide its growth.

Like executives build leadership teams with experts in every lane, you need a personal board of directors.

Your personal board of directors should include:

- someone who challenges your thinking and holds you accountable
- someone who opens doors and opens minds
- someone who tells you the truth, not only what you want to hear
- someone outside your industry who helps you see around corners
- someone who can speak to your financial growth, well-being, or mindset
- and yes, someone who understands visibility, communication, and personal brand strategy

The problem? Most people set their board once and never revisit it. Over time, they make decisions with perspectives that are outdated for where they want to go.

What they need isn't simply a refresh but an uplevel. Replacing "familiar" with "future-focused."

Your board reflects your direction. If it hasn't evolved, neither have you.

So, ask yourself:

- Who's still on my board because it's easy?
- Who's missing because I've been too focused on staying "loyal"?
- And who do I need now to help me think, lead, and act at the next level?

Change your board. Change your trajectory. Visibility shifts the moment your board does. Because visibility isn't built alone—it's built by the voices you let shape you.

CAREER VISIBILITY™ MOVE:

Rebuild your personal board of directors this month. Label each current member as value, gap, or misaligned. Then replace one gap with someone who pushes you to the next level. Make sure one seat is reserved for visibility and personal branding expertise.

REFLECT:

If your career is a business, who belongs on your leadership team right now—and who's missing from the table?

" Visibility isn't
performance.
It's presence. "

VISIBILITY TRUTH 34

The irony of leadership? You need to be seen.

Even the most capable leaders hesitate to fully show up. From the outside, they look like they've arrived. Inside? There's resistance—not to being known, but to being *seen*.

Because visibility disrupts comfort. It challenges unspoken rules about how you "should" lead, what's "too much" to say, and how much space you're allowed to take.

You've probably seen this play out. Brilliant leaders who shine with their teams but go quiet in the rooms where it matters most.

I saw it with a senior VP in a global tech company. She was a brilliant strategist who was exceptional at building high-performing teams.

But in senior leadership meetings, she consistently deferred credit to "her team." While they were indeed outstanding and essential to execution, she rarely articulated her own role in setting the vision, driving the strategy, and securing resources.

The result? She was seen as supportive, but not strategic. Collaborative, but not the driver.

When an opportunity for a major enterprise initiative emerged, she wasn't tapped. Leadership didn't fully connect her to the strategic outcomes she had, in fact, orchestrated.

Your leadership will only grow as far as your presence is felt.

The second-guessing is real:

- "Will they think I am taking all the credit?"
- "Am I sharing too much?"
- "What if I can't control how it's received?"

But at this level, holding back is expensive—not only for you but for the people counting on your clarity, your leadership, and your presence.

Your voice carries weight. Your experience carries wisdom. Your presence carries visibility—*when you let it.*

Visibility grows when others see both the "what" and the "who" behind the success.

CAREER VISIBILITY™ MOVE:

Balance team recognition with ownership. Share the win by naming your vision, decisions, and leadership role. Then credit your team for execution.

REFLECT:

Where have you been giving away too much credit, and how could you frame your contributions so your leadership is seen as clearly as your team's results?

"Live your story now. Don't just leave a legacy."

VISIBILITY TRUTH 35

Your legacy isn't what you leave behind—it's the story you make visible now.

At a private rooftop party in New York, I met the obituary writer for *The New York Times.* Within minutes, we realized we were in the same line of work: telling people's stories.

The difference? He works with the stories people leave behind. I work with people while they're still living theirs—helping them define how they want their leadership to be experienced, remembered, and talked about in rooms they're not in.

This is why visibility while you're leading matters so much. His subjects can't change or add to the narrative anymore. My clients can.

Take one executive I worked with—a brilliant change agent inside his company. For years, his impact was buried in internal reports and quiet conversations.

Once he made his work visible beyond his company—connecting projects to business outcomes and sharing his perspective publicly—perception of his leadership shifted almost overnight. The story he was living became the story others were telling. That's the Visibility Effect, when what you've done begins to ripple outward, shaping how others see you, remember you, and repeat your story.

Too many leaders leave that story to chance, letting others piece it together from scattered impressions, incomplete context, or a single snapshot in time.

That's how remarkable work gets overlooked, and how leadership impact gets erased from the record.

Visibility writes the record. Don't leave yours blank.

Make sure it tells your brilliance—one you can claim.

CAREER VISIBILITY™ MOVE:

Write your legacy statement, not as a eulogy but as a record of the difference you've already made. Capture the accomplishments, impact, and through-line that define your leadership so far. Shine a light on it now. Speak it, share it, and connect it to the bigger picture.

REFLECT:

What's the difference you've made that deserves to be celebrated now, and how will you make sure it's seen?

_____

_____

_____

_____

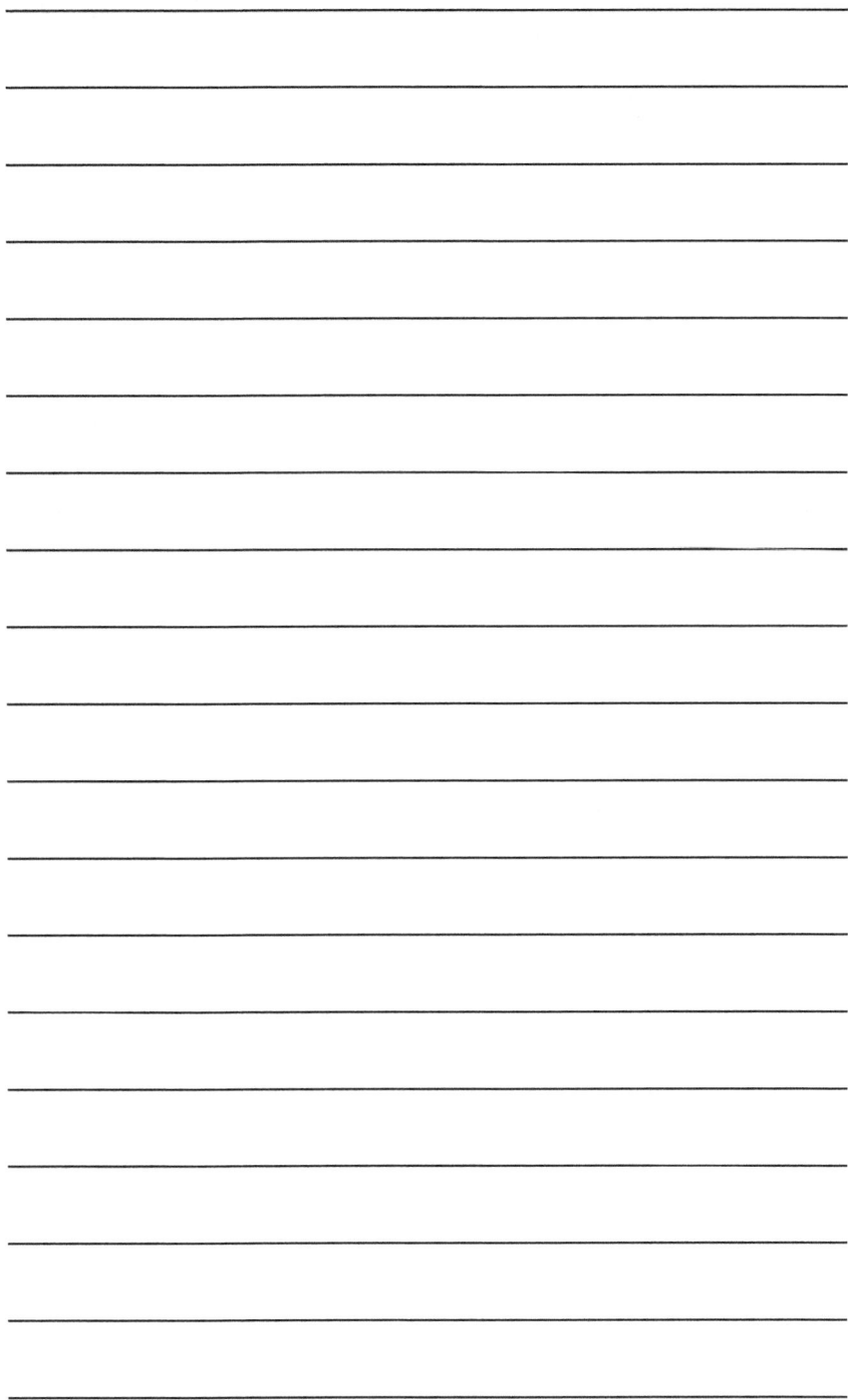

&& Make your presence felt so your absence is noticed. &&

VISIBILITY TRUTH 36

Your impact should be visible even after you've moved on.

I f you won the lottery tomorrow and sailed off on a world cruise, would people feel the gap you left? Would the systems, results, and reputation you built speak for you long after you stepped away?

In my consulting work, I build learning functions where none existed, embedding processes, developing talent, and creating structures that sustain over time. Sometimes that means I work myself out of a role. But when an organization needs to build again, they call me.

When you design for continuity, you also design for career longevity. You become the person known for building what lasts.

Visibility that lasts isn't the spotlight you stand in. It's the legacy that stands without you.

CAREER VISIBILITY™ MOVE:

Create your continuity framework: the systems, relation-ships, and proof points that keep your impact alive when you're not in the room. Make sure the right people can name it, explain it, and point to you as the one who built it.

REFLECT:

If you stepped away tomorrow, what proof would remain of the value you created, and would anyone know it was yours?

_____

_____

_____

_____

_____

_____

_____

_____

_____

_____

_____

_____

❝ Visibility is momentum that multiplies. ❞

VISIBILITY TRUTH 37

Amplification Beats Accumulation.

S mart leaders know visibility isn't a solo act. Media outlets know this too. That's why they never publish once and walk away. They push the same story across print, podcasts, video, and social media because they understand how reach multiplies when it spreads.

Inside organizations, it works the same way. Your story has to live on more than one channel, in more than one voice, if you want to build amplification waves that last.

I had a client, a corporate training leader, who built visibility into a leadership program. Participants earned digital badges they could share on LinkedIn. A Learner Spotlight series ran on the intranet, with short testimonials about their learning experience and growth. Managers showcased participants and cascaded stories in team meetings. One program, many waves. The result wasn't only learning impact—it became a visibility engine for the participants, the function, and the organizational culture.

Another client amplified her team's projects by submitting them for industry awards. Over a decade, she earned at least one major win a year. Each award multiplied impact:

press coverage, recruiting buzz, a stronger reputation inside her company, and even a platform for her as a sought-after industry speaker. Winning didn't just validate the work. It amplified it. Her team wasn't simply delivering. They were riding a wave of visibility that lifted her, her people, and her brand.

Here's the big shift: Amplification isn't self-serving. It's multichannel and multi-beneficial.

Every successfully amplified story asks: Who else should ride this wave with me? Who else benefits when this is seen, shared, and celebrated?

Amplification beats accumulation—because waves carry farther when others ride them with you.

CAREER VISIBILITY™ MOVE:

Take one result and amplify it three ways: through leaders, internal platforms, and external recognition. Don't stop at the result. Make a wave.

REFLECT:

What story of yours deserves to ripple across the org? Who else can benefit by riding the wave with you?

_____

_____

_____

_____

_____

“ Momentum
is built in
the timing. **”**

VISIBILITY TRUTH 38

Leave them wanting more.
Pivot before you peak.

G reat careers, like great performances, are remembered for timing. Step off too late, and the applause dies out. Step away at the right moment, or step back in with something new, and the spotlight follows you.

Reliability earns trust. But visibility is built on evolution, the fresh headline that keeps people watching.

One of my clients, a marketing director, nailed a launch so successful it could have defined her forever as the "launch woman" with one playbook. But she refused to be typecast. She pivoted while still in the spotlight: She raised her hand for a new product launch, reframed her skills, and reintroduced herself as more than a one-hit wonder. That move shifted her from specialist in one lane to versatile headliner—exactly the kind of leader executives wanted center stage for every major initiative.

Another client, a finance professional, took the opposite approach. Year after year, he delivered flawless reports. Reliable, yes. But consistency without refresh becomes wallpaper. He broke through only when he led a digital finance project that created real-time forecasting dashboards. Suddenly, leaders weren't waiting months for history—they were steering the business on live numbers. That pivot kept the spotlight on him—now as future-focused, not just keeping the financial score but setting the tempo for the organization.

Momentum isn't built by doing more of the same. It's built by evolving while you're still at the top.

Visibility isn't about holding the stage. It's about knowing when to set the stage for what's next.

CAREER VISIBILITY™ MOVE:

Identify one area where your work has already peaked. Decide your next move now—expand it, evolve it, or exit it—and let the spotlight follow you.

REFLECT:

Where in your career have you stayed too long at the summit? What would it look like to pivot while the spotlight is still on you?

_____

_____

_____

_____

_____

_____

" The AI train
has left
the station.
All aboard. **"**

VISIBILITY TRUTH 39

AI won't take your job, but someone who knows how to use it will.

A I isn't just about writing emails faster. It's about spotting opportunities, making smarter decisions, and proving you can adapt before the market forces you to. Staying visible means staying relevant, and nothing dates you faster than ignoring the tools that are reshaping your industry.

The people who will thrive aren't the ones avoiding it, or worse, using it in secret as if being AI-capable is something to hide. They're the ones riding the curve, shaping where it goes, and deciding how it works for them.

If you're in sales or business development, AI can help you map markets, predict client needs, and personalize outreach at scale. In marketing, it can turn raw data into actionable insight.

And that's only the beginning. Whatever your function, AI isn't about doing your job for you—it's about amplifying how you think and deliver. The question isn't whether it applies to your role—it's whether you'll be visible using it.

A CEO isn't spending hours training chatbots; they're steering the organization toward AI-driven strategy. They're asking: How can AI accelerate decision-making, create new revenue streams, or transform the client experience? They set the vision, allocate resources, and put guardrails in place to ensure responsible results. Their visibility isn't in the code—it's in the strategy.

Bottom line: You don't have to be a CEO to think like one. Whether you manage a team, run a project, or deliver as an individual contributor, the same lens applies: How can AI help you deliver smarter, faster, more valuable outcomes in your world?

The professionals who lean in now will be the ones people turn to later, not only for their output but for their foresight.

Whether you're an individual contributor or a senior executive, AI fluency signals adaptability. It tells the market, your employer, and your clients you're not just keeping up—you're ahead.

Adaptability is magnetic. In the learning and development world, we call it learning agility—the ability and willingness to learn, unlearn, and relearn at speed in changing circumstances. It's not simply reacting to change. It's anticipating, absorbing new information quickly, and applying it in new situations. It's a blend of **self-awareness, curiosity, flexibility, application,** and **resilience.**

For Career Visibility™, learning agility signals to decision-makers one thing: You're not just keeping pace—you're keeping ahead.

When the train leaves the station, you want to be seen not just onboard but helping to chart the route.

The future won't wait. And neither should your visibility.

CAREER VISIBILITY™ MOVE:

Shape where AI goes in your world. Find one way this month to use AI to improve your results, speed, or strategy. Document the win and share it with the right audience.

REFLECT:

Who are the one to three decision-makers or influencers who should know you're using AI, and how will you make sure they see it?

_____

_____

_____

_____

_____

_____

_____

_____

_____

_____

_____

"Skills can be taught. Mindset is trained."

VISIBILITY TRUTH 40

The ultimate career superpower isn't technical—it's mental.

Every pivot, promotion, or reintroduction comes down to this: Mindset outweighs mechanics. You can have the perfect résumé or portfolio, but if you show up tentative, apologetic, or uncertain, you'll make yourself invisible at the exact moment you need to be seen.

A confident, growth-oriented mindset shifts how you show up—in interviews, in meetings, in negotiations, in the day-to-day moments when visibility is built or lost. At the core of that mindset is your self-talk—the first story you tell yourself before you speak. The story you run in your head is the story others end up seeing. Change that, and you change how visible your readiness and resilience become when things don't go according to plan.

Research backs this up: Optimism fuels persistence. Believing you can influence outcomes keeps you visible in the room—because you speak up, stay engaged, and don't disappear when challenges hit. That career stamina is a visibility advantage no credential can replace.

Mindset makes you visible.

The people who win in careering aren't always the ones with the longest list of credentials. They're the ones who choose their mindset deliberately, over and over again, especially when it's hardest.

Two people can have the same technical skills. The one with the stronger mindset—curiosity, confidence, and the belief they belong—will not only be seen but remembered.

Mindset shows up in your tone, your risks, and your follow-up. It's the difference between being overlooked and being invited back. It's what makes people say "We need them in the next meeting" or "That's who should lead this project."

For Career Visibility™, mindset isn't just fuel—it's the ignition switch.

It doesn't start with what you do—it starts with what you tell yourself.

CAREER VISIBILITY™ MOVE:

Audit your self-talk this week. When a challenge or setback shows up, notice your first thought, then reframe it into a question that opens possibility.

REFLECT:

What self-talk shift would make your visibility impossible to ignore?

_____

_____

_____

❝ If you're not willing to risk being wrong, you'll never stand out for being right. ❞

VISIBILITY TRUTH 41

Playing it safe won't get you seen.

Think about the last time you sat in a meeting where everyone agreed, or at least pretended to. The presentation ended, heads nodded, and the decision was "locked."

But no one asked the hard question. No one challenged the gap in the plan.

And here's the thing: The person who does challenge it—with a well-placed question, an insight others missed, or a different angle—instantly shifts the room. They become memorable, trusted, and visible.

Safe players wait for permission. Visible players create moments.

They're not reckless, just willing to risk being wrong to stay relevant.

Whether you're an analyst spotting a data pattern that changes the forecast, a marketer suggesting a strategy the competition hasn't touched, or a leader questioning a direction that doesn't fit the vision, you're signaling that you think beyond your job description. You're not simply in the meeting. You're moving it.

Safety is invisible. Visibility gets remembered.

CAREER VISIBILITY™ MOVE:

Pinpoint one place this week where you've been playing it safe—in a meeting, on a project, or in your outreach. Take one visible, thoughtful risk, then track how it changes the way others engage with you.

REFLECT:

What's one bold move you could make this week that would put your visibility in motion?

_____

_____

_____

_____

_____

_____

_____

_____

_____

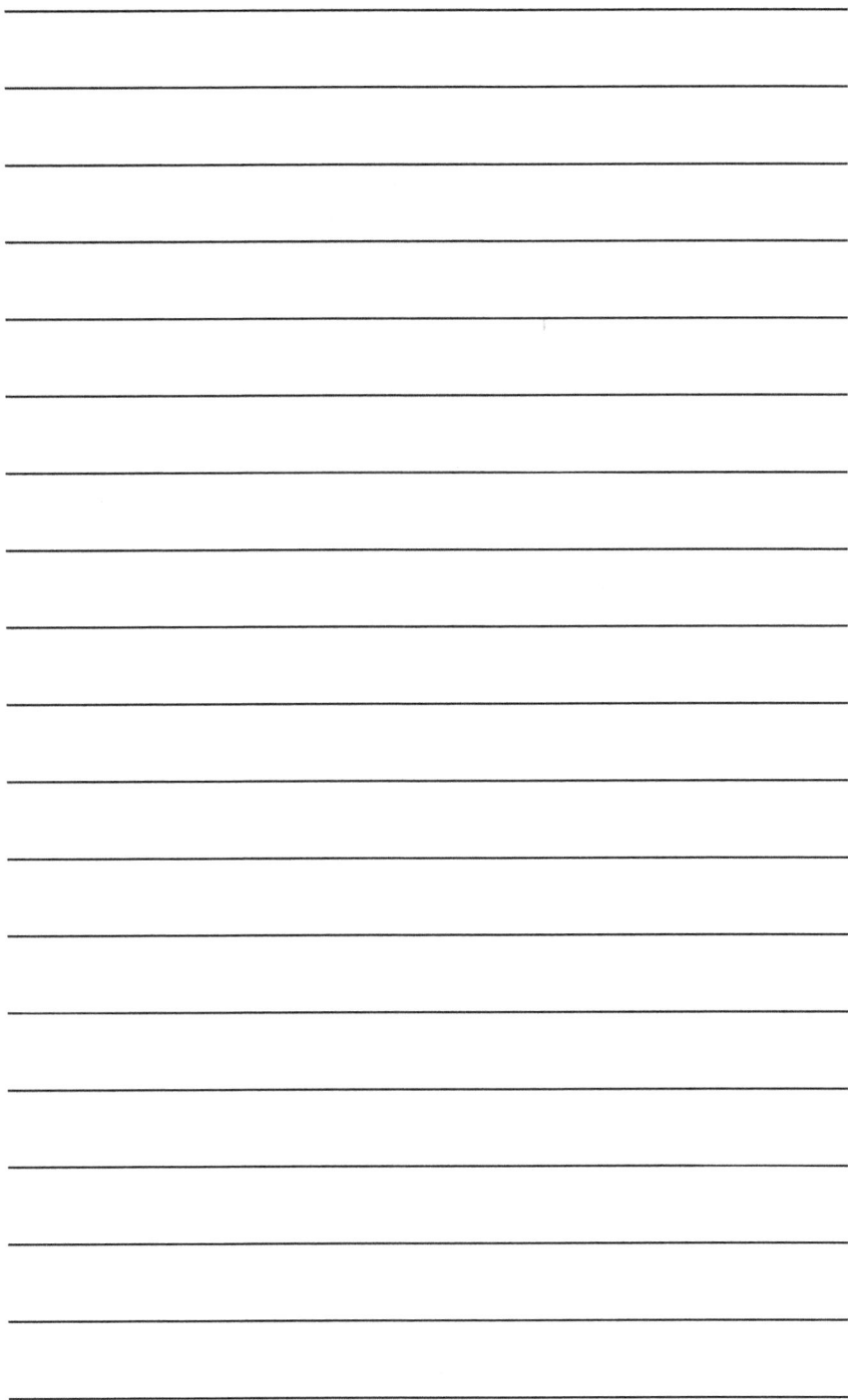

66 Visibility
favors the bold. 99

VISIBILITY TRUTH 42

Get visible. That's how you get ready.

S aying yes before you feel ready is how you *get* ready —and how you gain clarity. Visibility is the only real preparation.

When a newly minted consultant—fresh from a successful corporate career—was invited to be a guest on an industry-leading podcast, she almost said no.

Not because she didn't value the platform but because running her own business felt different. The confidence she'd had inside an organization suddenly felt shakier with her own name on the shingle.

Visibility feels different when you're backed by a corporate brand than when you *are* the brand. And when your name is on the line, it takes **boldness** to step forward anyway.

Whether you're behind a Fortune 500 logo or your own, visibility matters just as much. And the courage to claim it counts even more when it's only your name in lights.

She thought about "perfect timing," the "right" case study, the "ideal" story to share. But clarity doesn't come from waiting. It comes from stepping in, showing up, and letting your voice be heard.

Because every yes puts you in rooms—in real life or virtual—where people start associating your name with bold contributions and leadership. And the more you're seen in those spaces, the more often the next opportunity finds you instead of you chasing it.

Opportunities don't reward readiness. They reward **bold visibility.**

CAREER VISIBILITY™ MOVE:

Say yes to one visibility opportunity this quarter, even if it feels premature. A panel, a podcast, a high-profile meeting. Then prepare like it's your launch moment.

REFLECT:

What opportunity would you say yes to if you trusted boldness, not timing, to be your visibility advantage?

_____

_____

_____

_____

_____

_____

_____

“ Visibility rewards
the present,
not the perfect. ”

VISIBILITY TRUTH 43

Missing the room
is missing the moment.

My client, an early careerist in hospitality sales, was invited to join a respected industry panel. The subject wasn't her exact sales lane, so she passed. *"Better to wait until the topic fits,"* she thought.

What she didn't realize was that customer experience, and the unique lens hospitality brings to it, is a competitive advantage in any industry.

She could have stood out by bringing fresh examples, a different language of service, and an approach to client relationships her cross-industry peers didn't have.

Instead, the panel went ahead without her. Photos were posted, posts were shared, her peers were tagged, new connections formed, and competitors' voices shaped the conversation.

The audience now associated those names, not hers, with the topic.

In her corporate role, she had always been in the mix. Her presence was expected. But in the fast-moving cycle of conferences, webinars, and panels, **absence is a quiet eraser.** People don't remember why you weren't there. They simply remember who was.

And when the posts, photos, and tags rolled out, the FOMO hit hard.

Declining that panel didn't just cost her a microphone. It cost her the ripple effect—the visibility she could have multiplied for her brand, and her company's brand, by being part of the dialogue in real time.

I was recently invited to a panel on fractional leadership. At first, I pushed back. The other panelists were business owners who placed fractional talent. I was a practitioner. Different lens, different audience—or so I thought.

The moderator insisted my voice was needed—and she was right. My real-world experience rounded out the dialogue, and the conversation was far richer because of it.

Afterward, people reached out to say my perspective was the part they remembered and benefited from.

Had I written myself out, I would have erased myself from the opportunity and the impact.

Your perspective is your visibility. The one thing no one else can bring. The one thing that can shift the conversation.

Visibility changes everything—if you know how to use it.

CAREER VISIBILITY™ MOVE:

Before you pass, ask, *"Can I credibly contribute something valuable here?"* If the answer is yes—even if it's not your deepest lane—take the seat.

REFLECT:

When was the last time you watched the conversation happen without you? How did it feel when the posts, photos, and tags rolled out?

_____

_____

_____

_____

_____

_____

_____

_____

_____

_____

_____

_____

_____

" A title parks you.
A career brand
moves you. **"**

VISIBILITY TRUTH 44

Your personal brand is the engine.
Visibility is the ignition.
Without both, your career stalls.

P ush the button. Turn the key. Even the best engine
stays in park without ignition.
And that's exactly what happens when you lead
with your job title.

"I'm a project manager."
"I'm a third-year associate in M&A."
"I manage the top client accounts for the firm."

All safe. All accurate. All invisible.

Titles serve HR. They're how companies slot you into a job
family, determine your pay band, and manage their hierarchy.
Titles don't serve you. They don't differentiate your value.
They don't tell your story. They don't make you visible.
That's why inside *The Branding Room*™, I don't let clients hide behind titles. We excavate your real brand with
three questions:

1. What value do you create?
2. Why is that important to you?
3. Why is that important to your organization?

One client, a managing director in finance, had been introducing herself the same way for years: "I manage the top client accounts for the firm."

The problem? There were 136 other client account managers in the company. Nothing set her apart.

And without a clear brand, she wasn't visible; she was a head count.

A title makes you interchangeable. A brand makes you unforgettable.

When we pressed into the three questions, the fog lifted. What she created wasn't just "managing accounts." It was trust, protection. And risk management.

Her new message became "I help global investors safeguard their portfolios by identifying risk others miss—and that's how we protect both performance and trust."

That's the shift. Titles explain your role. Your brand explains your value. And that's the visible differentiator people remember.

Once she started using that brand messaging—in meetings, on panels, and in the way she followed up—she stopped sounding like one of 136. She became the one people remembered, repeated, and referred.

She didn't change her title. She didn't need to. While titles slot you in, personal brands set you apart.

Visibility makes sure everyone knows the difference.

CAREER VISIBILITY™ MOVE:

Answer the three brand questions in writing this week. Then introduce yourself without a title. Lead with what you *do*, not what you're *called*.

REFLECT:

If the only thing people knew about you was your title, what would they miss, and what do you want them to remember instead?

_____

_____

_____

_____

_____

_____

_____

_____

_____

_____

_____

"Serendipity is optional. Visibility is intentional."

VISIBILITY TRUTH 45

Your elevator moment didn't vanish.
It just went virtual.

Before COVID-19, careers moved in the margins—the ride with a senior leader, the hallway chat, or the impromptu breakroom drop-by. Serendipity once opened doors. Not anymore.

In a hybrid, scheduled world, visibility moments haven't disappeared—they've shifted. You have to spot them, and you have to create them.

This is why your elevator pitch still matters. Only now, the "elevator" might be a Zoom waiting room, a Slack thread, or the first two minutes of a quarterly meeting. And when the door opens, you can't ramble. You need to land it.

The three Cs of a powerful pitch: Confidence. Clarity. Concise. That's how leaders think. No babble. No backstory. Just bullet points that prove you get what matters.

As a global head of learning, I had a dotted line into the Fortune 500 COO. When she was prepping for her townhalls, I didn't only hand out data and long success stories. I gave her soundbites; sharp lines tied to culture, collaboration, and learning. The result—the Visibility Effect in action. She looked crisp. My L&D team looked strategic. And our impact got airtime at the highest levels.

And here's what I see in my Women in LeadHERship™ program: Junior and mid-career professionals often think visibility means talking more. It doesn't. It means speaking with intention. Tailor to your audience. Cut the fluff. When you speak to an executive: Be brief. Be brilliant. Be gone.

Even the origin of the elevator pitch proves the point. In the nineteenth century, Elisha Otis unveiled his new brake system not with a lecture but with a stunt. He stood on an open platform elevator at the World's Fair, ordered the rope cut, and let the crowd gasp as the platform dropped—until his brake stopped it cold. One move. One second. Everyone remembered.

Later, Hollywood screenwriters coined the term "elevator pitch" because an elevator ride gave them only sixty seconds to sell a film idea.

Both examples underline the same truth: Visibility moments are short—and unforgettable.

Stop waiting for the elevator ride. Make your own. And be ready when the door opens.

Serendipity isn't a strategy. Visibility is.

CAREER VISIBILITY™ MOVE:

Craft a sixty-second business update using the three Cs: confidence, clarity, and conciseness. Keep a version ready for a virtual meeting, a senior leader intro, or a chance connection.

REFLECT:

If you had sixty seconds with someone who could change your career, what would you say, and would it stick?

❝ Don't confuse flexibility with invisibility. ❞

VISIBILITY TRUTH 46

Visibility that depends on one person isn't visibility —it's vulnerability.

Fractional leaders. Contractors. Consultants. Portfolio professionals. The work model changes; the visibility rules don't. Modern fractional work isn't just a trendy rebrand of freelancing—it's embedded, accountable leadership inside lean orgs that delivers enterprise outcomes.

Here's the trap: You deliver results, but only your sponsoring executive sees them. Then there's a reorg, a downsizing, or your sponsor exits, and suddenly your work disappears with them. Flexibility without multi-threaded visibility is career risk.

In the Career Visibility Studio™, I guided a brilliant client in creating an Enterprise Visibility Plan when she realized this truth: If your sponsor isn't always in the room, your visibility can't depend on them.

We built it around three visibility moves:

- **Widen the net:** Identify one to three stakeholders who can see and speak to your impact.
- **Show the score:** Send a monthly "results receipt" that proves outcomes, not activity.
- **Claim the mic:** Deliver a ninety-second win in leadership forums that ties directly to business priorities.

When her sponsor was moved in a reorg, my client didn't disappear. Finance cited her results. HR pulled her into a new project. Peers vouched for her. Her contract wasn't just extended—it was expanded.

CAREER VISIBILITY™ MOVE:

Don't tie your visibility to one person; translate it so it sticks across the enterprise by recasting it as a business result.

REFLECT:

If your sponsor left tomorrow, who else could name your outcomes and repeat your name in the room?

_____

_____

_____

_____

_____

_____

❝ The last story they tell about you is the one that lasts. **❞**

VISIBILITY TRUTH 47

First impressions count.
Final impressions define.

Executives spend months prepping for onboarding and almost no time prepping for offboarding. Yet how you resign may be one of the most visibility-defining moves of your career.

A CFO client had already secured her next dream role. We built a resignation plan—because at her level, the goal wasn't just notification; it was reputation, relationships, and continuity.

Why exit visibility matters:

- Relationships: Don't leave people scrambling. Protect trust you may need later.
- Reputation: A polished transition signals judgment, foresight, and maturity.
- References: Leaders who see you exit well become future advocates.
- Opportunities: Strong finishes keep doors open for referrals, boards, and boomerangs.

She left more than notice. She left a plan:

- Clarity: Professional letter with decision and timeline.
- Gratitude: Specific recognition of people, partnerships, and milestones.
- Achievements: Documented contributions tied to business outcomes.
- Continuity: Handoffs, successor input, and knowledge transfer to protect momentum.

She exited—but she didn't vanish.

She left a legacy of visibility.

Her resignation became the final proof point of her leadership: accountable, professional, and visible. Continuity was intact. Clients and teams were reassured. The business never missed a beat. And the vibe on her last day? "We're going to feel this"—not "Finally, she's gone."

I've seen both. So have you.

The difference isn't just the exit. It's the combination of exceptional work and exceptional relationships that keeps you visible to the very end.

Resignation isn't the finale. Visibility sets up the sequel.

Another senior client exited with the same gravitas and discipline: clean handoffs, visible outcomes, and generous credit. Eighteen months later, after a reorg, the board needed a steady hand. They called her back—bigger scope, better comp, and stronger seat.

Visibility doesn't end when you walk out the door. You may be gone, but your visibility lingers.

CAREER VISIBILITY™ MOVE:

Your last act should be visible. Don't just resign—script your last chapter. Leave results and reputation visible when you exit.

REFLECT:

If you exited tomorrow, what would stay visible after you left?

_____

_____

_____

_____

_____

_____

_____

_____

_____

_____

“ The moment
you claim
your agency,
everything
else expands. ”

VISIBILITY TRUTH 48

Agency is the lever.
Visibility is the launch.

Engagement is an inside job, and visibility is how people know you've claimed it.

I once heard Matthew Knowles, Beyoncé's father, speak to a group of entrepreneurs. He said, "Stop thinking outside the box. Think like the box has no lines."

That landed hard. Because when you erase the lines, you don't only create expansion. You create visibility.

People can actually see you operating beyond the constraints of your role or organization, and that's the spark that shifts a career from quiet competence to undeniable presence.

High achievers forget this. They manage deliverables as if that's their only job. It isn't. Managing your career is the other job, and managing your career starts with agency: the decision to take control of your trajectory instead of waiting for someone else to map it. Sure, your manager plays a role. Your organization plays a role. But engagement, like visibility, isn't handed to you. It's something you claim.

One of my longtime clients, a customer service manager, had risen quickly but hit a wall. The work was mastered, the spark was gone, and she was waiting for her company to "figure her out." But no one was going to.

I encouraged her to claim her agency and start thinking and creating outside the lines by taking a leadership role in a professional association, volunteering for projects that energized her, and investing in her own development.

The difference was visible. Her energy was palpable. You could see it in her walk, in the way her voice carried more conviction, and in her sharper style. Even on Zoom, she showed up differently, with camera on, making direct eye contact, and leaning forward. She asked bolder questions and offered ideas that cut across departments. She wasn't simply "doing the work"—she was being seen doing it differently.

Agency sparked the engagement shift. Visibility made it visible.

And that visibility changed everything. Suddenly, she wasn't the manager who was "stuck." She was the one bringing energy, perspective, and momentum.

Research backs this. Employees who drive their own development are 3.6x more likely to be engaged and 23% more likely to be promoted than peers who wait for the company to do it for them (source: Gallup / CCL).

Engagement sparks. Agency ignites. Visibility amplifies. That's how careers accelerate.

CAREER VISIBILITY™ MOVE:

Find your spark outside the lines. Bring it back to work and make it visible.

REFLECT:

Are you letting your role box you in, or are you erasing the lines to claim your agency, your engagement, and your visibility?

_____

_____

_____

_____

_____

_____

_____

_____

_____

_____

_____

_____

_____

_____

_____

" Your network isn't
your net worth.
Your visibility is. **"**

VISIBILITY TRUTH 49

Hard work makes you competent. Networks make you visible.

I t's not who you know. It's whose life is better because they know you.

That's the heart of visibility.

Real networking isn't transactional. It's transformational.

It's not about contacts collected, handshakes tallied, or names in a database. It's about impact.

Whose decisions are sharper because of your perspective? Whose work is stronger because of your input? Whose opportunities expanded because you showed up?

Here's the reality: By now, 80% of your capability is assumed. It's the other 20%—visibility—that separates the overlooked from the accelerated.

One of my clients, an emerging leader at a retail brand, discovered this when she shifted from execution to contribution.

She connected her insights to peers' marketing campaigns. She spotted opportunities leaders had missed. She didn't only do what was asked. She reframed decisions that shaped the business. She didn't only keep up with internal work. She brought in external trends and fresh insights from the market that gave her team a competitive edge.

And leaders noticed. Her work didn't just build her reputation. It built her network, and that network opened doors.

Senior leaders pulled her into rooms she'd never been invited to before. They looked to her as a thought partner, not simply a solid performer.

In short, she multiplied value and, with it, her visibility soared.

That's the shift. Visibility through contribution, not just task completion. It's being remembered because you made someone's work, thinking, or life better.

Visibility, like networking, is a lifestyle. It's how your value moves into new rooms, new relationships, and new opportunities.

Generosity isn't soft. It's a strategy.

Add value everywhere—in your work and your network.

Visibility grows where value flows.

CAREER VISIBILITY™ MOVE:

Each week, add value to someone in your network: Share an article, make an intro, or check in without an agenda.

REFLECT:

Are you treating networking as a transaction—or as a lifestyle that makes you visible, valuable, and unforgettable?

_____

_____

_____

"" Your career won't be defined by a single win. It will be defined by how consistently you show up, get seen, and stay remembered. ""

VISIBILITY TRUTH 50

Visibility isn't a flash.
It's sustainability.

Flashes fade. Visibility doesn't.

Yes, it may ebb and flow. Sometimes you're in the spotlight, and sometimes you're behind the scenes, but when you build it with intention, it never disappears. It compounds.

That's the difference between a *moment* and a *momentum*.

Sustained visibility isn't one lightning strike—it's the series of moments you choose, stack, and sustain.

Too many professionals bet on the moment—the promotion cycle, the big presentation, or the "perfect" project. They shine once, then fade.

I've seen it in careers. I've seen it in leadership programs. Momentum gets lost. Impact gets forgotten. The flavor-of-the-month disappears.

That's why I created the Career Visibility Studio™: to sustain visibility over time. To help leaders stop chasing one-off sparks and start building a rhythm of presence that compounds into reputation, opportunity, and voice.

One senior client saw this firsthand. After a high-profile town hall presentation, she was celebrated for weeks—and then forgotten.

When we worked together, she stopped relying on one big moment and built a cadence following up, contributing in industry forums, and mentoring visibly.

Over time, she wasn't only remembered for one event— she became known for sustained impact.

And that's the point. Visibility isn't a flash. It's a force. The flash gets attention. The force builds a legacy.

And that's *The Visibility Effect*.

CAREER VISIBILITY™ MOVE:

Choose one visibility habit you can sustain. Do it every week. Not loud. Just consistent. Over time, the rhythm will outlast the moment.

REFLECT:

Is your visibility fading with the flash or compounding with the momentum that builds careers?

_____

_____

_____

_____

_____

_____

Now You See It

You don't stumble into being seen. You choose it.

In the meetings where your voice already carries weight, you use it with purpose.

In the conversations where you're known for results, you expand the story of your value. In the moments when you're pivoting, plateauing, or aiming higher, you make your next move visible.

Visibility isn't a one-time moment. It's a daily practice of showing up—at every stage of success.

Now comes the Visibility Choice: the choice to act.

To keep showing up. To take visible steps that signal not only what you've done but who you're becoming.

The Visibility Effect isn't theory. It's your reality waiting to happen.

Each day, ask yourself: *What's one visible action I'll take today?* Then do it.

Because visibility doesn't change you. It reveals you. And that changes everything.

This book gave you the truths. Now it's your turn to claim them.

Commit to it. Sign it. Live it.

Career Visibility™ Commitment Pledge

✓ I commit to leading with clarity and conviction.

✓ I will make my value visible, my voice heard, and my impact undeniable.

✓ I choose the actions that shape my path and the visibility that accelerates it.

Sign here if you're in.

_____

Acknowledgments

To my family—for the encouragement, support, and endless patience. And to my husband, who kept me well-fed through every draft—your quiet care has always been visible.

To Ann Ward, who graciously allowed me to pilot the Career Visibility™ frameworks in her training programs—thank you for what began as a simple, offhand question: *"Do you know anyone who wants to write a book?"* That moment gave me the spark to say *yes*—and bring this book to life.

To my early champions at adm-Indicia Global—Joanne Prifti, who opened the doors and gave me the first platform to bring Career Visibility™ into the corporate world; and Mike Clarke, whose vision as executive sponsor helped make the programs possible. And to every program participant who engaged in Career Visibility™ coaching sessions—your willingness to put these ideas into action means everything.

To Phyllis Pavlovsky, my first manager and lifelong mentor—your steadfast encouragement has stayed with me always.

To every manager along the way—whether you promoted me, challenged me, or gave me opportunities to step up—each of you shaped my path.

To Lisa Umina, my publisher, and her team at Elite/Halo International—for believing in this project and bringing it to life with such heart.

To Angela Evans—whose calm presence and uncanny ability to anticipate what I needed before I even said it were indispensable.

To all my brilliant clients—your trust in me to guide your career journeys has inspired me in countless ways and fueled the evolution of this work.

And finally, to you, the reader—may these truths help you move forward with purpose, amplify your impact, and experience *The Visibility Effect*: accelerating your career, amplifying your voice, and making your value unmistakable.

Book Club Bonus:

Conversations That Make Visibility Real

C areer Visibility™ isn't just an individual advantage—it grows stronger when it's shared. Think of this as your *book club bonus*: a simple set of prompts to guide meaningful conversations, spark reflection, and inspire action. Use it on your own, in a book club, a peer group, or an Employee Resource Group (ERG).

For Individuals, ERGs, and Book Clubs

- Which truth hit hardest and why?
- Where have you seen this play out in your career (for better or worse)?
- What patterns or blind spots are you becoming more aware of?
- What's one Career Visibility™ move you'll try this week?
- What's your biggest takeaway from *The Visibility Effect* so far?

For Organizational Use (HR, Managers, Executives, and L&D)

- How can Career Visibility™ become part of how we grow and recognize talent?

- Which truths could we integrate into career development or succession planning?
- Where are we modeling visibility well, and where are we falling short?

How to Use These Prompts

Meet regularly (monthly works well), allow time for each voice, and close by having each participant commit to one visible action before the next conversation.

Author's Tip

Career Visibility™ grows stronger when it's shared. The more you talk about it, model it, and support it with others, the more it becomes part of how careers move forward—for you and those around you.

Ready to Go Deeper?

Get the complete Career Visibility™ Discussion Guide and Facilitator Notes

Take these conversations further with the complete Career Visibility™ Discussion Guide—a high impact resource featuring expanded prompts, facilitator notes, and group formats—that ignite meaningful dialogue, build a culture of visibility and growth, elevate talent conversations, strengthen career development, drive professional growth, turn insight into visible action, and boost engagement and retention while creating lasting career momentum.

*To access the full guide or explore how to bring it your organization, team, professional association, or book club, reach out to me **directly.***

Work With Me

I work with ambitious professionals and forward-thinking organizations to make careers, leaders, and teams visible where it matters most.

Workshops & Programs

- **Career Visibility™ Series:** Not just visible—unforgettable.
- **Women in LeadHERship™:** Rise with visibility.

One-on-One Coaching

- **Career Visibility™ Sessions:** Turn credibility into opportunity.
- **The Branding Room™:** Résumé, LinkedIn. Bios. Your story, your value, your personal brand promise.
- **Coach-on-Call:** On-demand career strategy. Real-time moves. Sustained momentum. Continuous visibility. Enduring relevance.

Speaking, Keynotes & Panels

Dynamic talks. Interactive breakouts—Visibility that inspires action. Signature Topics include:

- **The Visibility Effect**—discover the six pillars of Career Visibility™ for being seen, heard, and remembered.
- **The Visibility IQ™**—assess and elevate the one skill every successful career now depends on.
- **Visibility by Design**—design the moments, messages, and moves that make your impact undeniable.

- **The Visibility Advantage**™—How Organizations Grow and Keep Their Best People — Visibility as the driver of engagement, retention, and internal mobility.
- **The Future of Work Is Visible**™ — What it takes to thrive, lead, and stay relevant in the modern workplace.

Corporate Teams & Functions

Elevate your team's or function's visibility. Shift from service provider to strategic driver.

Stay Connected

✉ Email: **janet@wiseadvantages.com**

in linkedin.com/in/janetwiseadvantages

🌐 www.wiseadvantages.com

Visibility changes everything. Let's make it work for you.

It's your ultimate career advantage.

About the Author

Janet Wise, MS, HRD, is Chief Career Visibility™ Strategist and the creator of Career Visibility™, her proprietary framework designed to make professionals seen, heard, and valued. She is founder of The Branding Room™, The Career Visibility Studio™, and Women in LeadHERship™—platforms that have propelled ambitious professionals into the rooms and roles that matter.

For more than two decades, Janet has architected global learning, leadership, and career development inside Fortune 500 firms scaling award-winning enterprise-wide leadership programs and building functions that elevated leaders at every level. She has been at the talent table across industries, partnering with CEOs, executives, and HR leaders to identify, elevate, and prepare top talent. She knows this truth: **Exceptional performance is not enough to career forward. It takes vision—and it takes visibility.**

Today, as a Fractional CLO, she partners with organizations to establish learning functions and internal mobility strategies that keep both talent and businesses future-ready.

A frequent speaker, panelist, and moderator on Career Visibility™, women's leadership, and personal branding, Janet also serves the profession as an active advisor and former chapter president for the **Association for Talent Development (ATD)** Long Island.

Janet holds a master's degree in human resource development and advanced certifications in executive coaching, change management, media psychology, Positive Intelligence®, Seasons of Change®, and Best Year Yet®. Janet blends deep expertise with real-world experience to help people and organizations succeed.

She firmly believes: **You are the most important product you will ever market. Visibility changes everything. It turns recognition into opportunity and performance into influence.**

www.ingramcontent.com/pod-product-compliance
Lightning Source LLC
Chambersburg PA
CBHW071641200326
41519CB00012BA/2361